TEACHER'S PET PUBLICATIONS

LITPLAN TEACHER PACK
for
Maniac Magee
based on the book by
Jerry Spinelli

Written by
Barbara M. Linde, MA Ed.

© 1997 Teacher's Pet Publications
All Rights Reserved

This **LitPlan** for *Maniac Magee*
has been brought to you by Teacher's Pet Publications, Inc.

Copyright Teacher's Pet Publications 1997
11504 Hammock Point
Berlin MD 21811

Only the student materials in this unit plan may be reproduced. Pages such as worksheets and study guides may be reproduced for use in the purchaser's classroom. For any additional copyright questions, contact Teacher's Pet Publications.

www.tpet.com

TABLE OF CONTENTS *Maniac Magee*

Introduction	6
Unit Objectives	8
Unit Outline	9
Reading Assignment Sheet	10
Study Questions	13
Quiz/Study Questions (Multiple Choice)	27
Pre-Reading Vocabulary Worksheets	51
Lesson One (Introductory Lesson)	79
Oral Reading Evaluation Form	84
Writing Assignment 1	86
Writing Evaluation Form	87
Nonfiction Assignment Sheet	96
Writing Assignment 2	97
Writing Assignment 3	102
Extra Writing Assignments/Discussion ?s	104
Project Ideas	114
Vocabulary Review Activities	116
Unit Review Activities	117
Unit Tests	125
Unit Resource Materials	161
Vocabulary Resource Materials	183

FEW NOTES ABOUT THE AUTHOR

SPINELLI, JERRY 1941- Jerry Spinelli was born on February 1, 1941, in Norristown, Pennsylvania. While still a youngster, one of his poems about a hometown football team's victory was published in a local paper. This inspired him to consider a career as a writer. As an adult writer, he thought he should write about topics that would be interesting to adults. The publishers he approached were not interested in his work. After he married, he started writing about things his own children did. One incident, when his child ate some food he was saving for himself, was the inspiration for his first book, *Space Station Seventh Grade*.

Space Station Seventh Grade (Little, Brown, 1982) tells the daily life of Jason Herkimer. Jason deals with everyday incidents as well as serious issues such as his parents' divorce, and living with a stepfather. In the sequel, *Jason and Marceline* (Little, Brown, 1990), Jason and the trombone player, Marceline, develop a deeper, more caring, and romantic relationship.

Who Put That Hair in My Toothbrush? (Little, Brown, 1984) is the story of Megin and Greg, siblings who fight a lot but unite against a common threat. The story is told in first person, with chapters alternating between Megin and Greg.

Maniac Magee (Little, Brown, 1990) was the Newbery Medal winner in 1991. In this book, Spinelli deals with the absurdities of racism. Jeffrey Lionel Magee is a Caucasian boy who is orphaned at the age of three. He runs away from his aunt and uncle's tension-filled home, and lives with a succession of people. The first is a kind and loving black family. He leaves them when racist graffiti is sprayed on their home. Next he lives with an old man in the equipment room of the park, but the man dies. After that he lives with a racist, dysfunctional white family. Nicknamed Maniac because of his athletic feats, he tries to start better racial relationships between the blacks and whites. Maniac Magee also won the Boston Globe/Horn Book Award, 1990, American Library Association, 1991, and the D.C. Fisher Award, 1992.

Spinelli's other works include *Dump Days,* (Little, Brown, 1988), *The Bathwater Gang* (Little, Brown, 1990), *There's a Girl in My Hammerlock,* (Simon and Schuster, 1991), and *Fourth Grade Rats* (Scholastic, 1991.) He lives in Phoenixville, Pennsylvania.

THE NEWBERY MEDAL

The Newbery Medal is named in honor of John Newbery (1713-1767), a British publisher and bookseller in the 1700s. Newbery is known as the father of children's literature because he was the first to propose publishing books specifically for children. The award is presented each year by the American Library Association to the "author of the most distinguished contribution to American literature for children" published during the preceding year. The award was first given in 1922, and is awarded annually. The winning book receives the Newbery Medal and one or more runners-up are also recognized as honor books.

YEAR	TITLE	AUTHOR
1997	*The View from Saturday*	Elaine Konigsburg
1996	*The Midwife's Apprentice*	Karen Cushman
1995	*Walk Two Moons*	Sharon Creech
1994	*The Giver*	Lois Lowry
1993	*Missing May*	Cynthia Rylant
1992	*Shiloh*	Phyllis Reynolds Naylor
1991	*Maniac Magee*	Jerry Spinelli
1990	*Number the Stars*	Lois Lowry
1989	*Joyful Noise: Poems for Two Voices*	Paul Fleischman
1988	*Lincoln: A Photobiography*	Russell Freeman
1987	*The Whipping Boy*	Sid Fleischman
1986	*Sarah, Plain and Tall*	Patricia MacLachlan
1985	*The Hero and the Crown*	Robin McKinley
1984	*Dear Mr. Henshaw*	Beverly Cleary
1983	*Dicey's Song*	Cynthia Voight
1982	*A Visit To William Blake's Inn*	Nancy Willard
1981	*Jacob Have I Loved*	Katherine Ann Patterson
1980	*A Gathering of Days*	Joan W. Blos
1970	*Sounder*	William H. Armstrong
1960	*Onion John*	Joseph Krumgold
1950	*The Door in the Wall*	Marguerite de Angeli
1940	*Daniel Boone*	James Daugherty
1930	*Hitty, Her First Hundred Years*	Rachel Field
1922	*The Story of Mankind*	Hendrik Wilem van Loon

INTRODUCTION

This unit has been designed to develop students' reading, writing, thinking, listening and speaking skills through exercises and activities related to *Maniac Magee* by Jerry Spinelli. It includes twenty lessons, supported by extra resource materials.

The **introductory lesson** introduces students to one main theme of the novel, racial prejudice, through a bulletin board and a student participation activity. Following the introductory activity, students are given an explanation of how the activity relates to the book they are about to read.

The **reading assignments** are approximately twenty-five pages each; some are a little shorter while others are a little longer. Students have approximately 15 minutes of pre-reading work to do prior to each reading assignment. This pre-reading work involves reviewing the study questions for the assignment and doing some vocabulary work for 8 to 10 vocabulary words they will encounter in their reading.

The **study guide questions** are fact-based questions; students can find the answers to these questions right in the text. These questions come in two formats: short answer or multiple choice. The best use of these materials is probably to use the short answer version of the questions as study guides for students (since answers will be more complete), and to use the multiple choice version for occasional quizzes. It might be a good idea to make transparencies of your answer keys for the overhead projector.

The **vocabulary work** is intended to enrich students' vocabularies as well as to aid in the students' understanding of the book. Prior to each reading assignment, students will complete a two-part worksheet for approximately 8 to 10 vocabulary words in the upcoming reading assignment. Part I focuses on students' use of general knowledge and contextual clues by giving the sentence in which the word appears in the text. Students are then to write down what they think the words mean based on the words' usage. Part II gives students dictionary definitions of the words and has them match the words to the correct definitions based on the words' contextual usage. Students should then have an understanding of the words when they meet them in the text.

After each reading assignment, students will go back and formulate answers for the study guide questions. Discussion of these questions serves as a **review** of the most important events and ideas presented in the reading assignments.

After students complete extra discussion questions, there is a **vocabulary review** lesson which pulls together all of the separate vocabulary lists for the reading assignments and gives students a review of all of the words they have studied.

Following the reading of the book, two lessons are devoted to the **extra discussion questions/writing assignments**. These questions focus on interpretation, critical analysis and personal response, employing a variety of thinking skills and adding to the students' understanding of the novel. These questions are done as a **group activity**. Using the information they have acquired so far through individual work and class discussions, students get together to further examine the text and to brainstorm ideas relating to the themes of the novel.

The group activity is followed by a **reports and discussion** session in which the groups share their ideas about the book with the entire class; thus, the entire class gets exposed to many different ideas regarding the themes and events of the book.

There are three **writing assignments** in this unit, each with the purpose of informing, persuading, or having students express personal opinions. The first assignment is to **persuade**: students will try to persuade someone to perform a task or give the writer something. The second assignment is to **inform**: students will give information about a non-fiction topic related to *Maniac Magee*. The third assignment is to express a personal **opinion**: students will write Clerihew and acrostic poems based on the novel.

The **nonfiction reading assignment** is used as Writing Assignment #2. Students are required to read a piece of nonfiction related in some way to *Maniac Magee*. After reading their nonfiction pieces, students will fill out a worksheet on which they answer questions regarding facts, interpretation, criticism, and personal opinions. They will also write a short report on the information they researched. During one class period, students make **oral presentations** about the nonfiction pieces they have read. This not only exposes all students to a wealth of information, it also gives students the opportunity to practice **public speaking**.

The **review lesson** pulls together all of the aspects of the unit. The teacher is given four or five choices of activities or games to use which all serve the same basic function of reviewing all of the information presented in the unit.

The **unit test** comes in two formats: all multiple choice-matching-true/false or with a mixture of matching, short answer, and composition. As a convenience, two different tests for each format have been included.

There are additional **support materials** included with this unit. The **extra activities packet** includes suggestions for an in-class library, crossword and word search puzzles related to the novel, and extra vocabulary worksheets. There is a list of **bulletin board ideas** which gives the teacher suggestions for bulletin boards to go along with this unit. In addition, there is a list of **extra class activities** the teacher could choose from to enhance the unit or as a substitution for an exercise the teacher might feel is inappropriate for his/her class. **Answer keys** are located directly after the **reproducible student materials** throughout the unit. The student materials may be reproduced for use in the teacher's classroom without infringement of copyrights. No other portion of this unit may be reproduced without the written consent of Teacher's Pet Publications, Inc.

UNIT OBJECTIVES *Maniac Magee*

1. Through reading *Maniac Magee* students will analyze characters and their situations to better understand the themes of the novel.

2. Students will demonstrate their understanding of the text on four levels: factual, interpretive, critical, and personal.

3. Students will practice reading aloud and silently to improve their skills in each area.

4. Students will enrich their vocabularies and improve their understanding of the novel through the vocabulary lessons prepared for use in conjunction with it.

5. Students will answer questions to demonstrate their knowledge and understanding of the main events and characters in *Maniac Magee*.

6. Students will practice writing through a variety of writing assignments.

7. The writing assignments in this are geared to several purposes:
    a. To check the students' reading comprehension
    b. To make students think about the ideas presented by the novel
    c. To make students put those ideas into perspective
    d. To encourage critical and logical thinking
    e. To provide the opportunity to practice good grammar and improve students' use of the English language.

8. Students will read aloud, report, and participate in large and small group discussions to improve their public speaking and personal interaction skills.

UNIT OUTLINE *Maniac Magee*

1	2	3	4	5
Unit Intro Distribute Unit Materials	PVR 1-5 Study ?? 1-5	PVR 6-11 Oral Reading Evaluation	Writing Assignment #1 Persuade Study ?? 6-11	Minilesson: Cause & Effect PVR 12-16 Study ?? 12-16
6	7	8	9	10
Minilesson: Simile & Metaphor PVR 17-21 Study?? 17-21	Quiz 1-21 PVR 22-26 Study ?? 22-26	Minilesson: Character Traits Study ?? 22-26 PVR 27-32	Writing Conference PVR 33-37	Study?? 33-37 Writing Assignment #2/ Non-Fiction Information
11	12	13	14	15
PVR 38-41	Study ?? 38-41 PVR 42-46	Minilesson: Story Map Study ??42-46	Writing Assignment #3 Personal Opinion	Extra Discussion Questions
16	17	18	19	20
Project/ Group Work	Vocabulary Review	Unit Review	Test	Non-Fiction Assignment Presentations

Key: P = Preview Study Questions   V = Vocabulary Work   R = Read

READING ASSIGNMENT SHEET *Maniac Magee*

Date to be Assigned	Chapters	Completion Date
	Chapters 1-5	
	Chapters 6-11	
	Chapters 12-16	
	Chapters 17-21	
	Chapters 22-26	
	Chapters 27-32	
	Chapters 33-37	
	Chapters 38-41	
	Chapters 42-46	

STUDY QUESTIONS

SHORT ANSWER STUDY QUESTIONS *Maniac Magee*

Chapters 1-5
1. What was Maniac's real name?
2. With whom did Maniac live, and why? What was his life there like? How long did he live that way?
3. What happened the night of the musical?
4. Where did he go when he left Hollidaysburg? How long did it take him to get there?
5. What did people see and hear when they saw Maniac on his first day in town?
6. Who was the first person Maniac talked with? Describe their meeting.
7. Who lived in the East End? Who lived in the West End?
8. Describe Maniac's meeting with Brian Denehy and James "Hands" Down.
9. Describe what happened at Finsterwald's house.

Chapters 6-11
1. Describe dinner at the Pickwell home. How did the children know it was time for dinner? How many family members ate there?
2. After dinner, Jeffrey ran somewhere. Where did he run? Why were the Pickwell kids surprised?
3. Describe John McNab. Why wasn't the rest of the league any match for him?
4. Describe the play between Jeffrey as batter and John McNab as pitcher.
5. How did Jeffrey get the name "Maniac"?
6. Where did Jeffrey sleep?
7. How did he like Amanda's book?
8. What did John McNab try to do to get even? What happened?
9. What unthinkable thing did Maniac do when he met Mars Bar Thompson? Why was it so unthinkable?
10. Describe the scene with Maniac's book.
11. What happened while Maniac was trying to find Amanda's house?

Chapters 12-16
1. How did Maniac end up staying with the Beale family?
2. What was "the miracle on Sycamore Street"?
3. Describe some of the other changes in the Beale household.
4. What was Maniac's allergy?
5. How did Maniac feel about his new life?
6. How did the East End kids find out Jeffrey was "that Maniac kid?"
7. What was Jeffrey afraid of losing, and why?
8. How did the kids in the East End react to Maniac?
9. How was Maniac blind?
10. What did Manic think about skin color?

Chapters 17-21

1. What happened to Maniac while the children were playing in the fire hydrant water?
2. What was on the wall of the Beales' house a few days later? How did the family react? How did Maniac react?
3. Amanda and Maniac had an argument. What did Amanda say that she felt sorry for?
4. Describe Cobble's Knot. Where was it? What was the prize for untying it?
5. Why did Amanda want Maniac to untie the knot?
6. Did Maniac untie the knot?
7. What did Maniac and Amanda discover about the confetti? What did Maniac do?
8. Describe the way Maniac walked out of town.

Chapters 22-26

1. Where was Maniac living?
2. Who found Maniac? Where did they go? What did they do?
3. What did they do after Grayson bought the Krimpets?
4. Where did Maniac say he wanted to stay?
5. Grayson asked Maniac about school. What was Maniac's answer?
6. What kind of questions did Grayson ask Maniac?
7. What did Grayson invite Maniac to do, and what was Maniac's reply?
8. What did Maniac discover about Grayson's past?
9. How did Maniac and Grayson begin spending their afternoons?
10. How was Maniac keeping up with his education?
11. What did Grayson ask Maniac to do?

Chapters 27-32

1. Maniac taught Grayson to read. When did they work? What kind of books did he use? What was difficult, and what was easy for Grayson?
2. What was the first book Grayson read? How did Maniac react?
3. How was the room different than when Maniac first moved in?
4. How did Maniac and Grayson spend Thanksgiving?
5. What did Maniac do with the paint?
6. What did they do at Christmas? Where was Grayson living?
7. What did they do on Christmas Day? What presents did they give each other?
8. What did Maniac do when he discovered Grayson was dead?
9. Describe the funeral.

Chapters 33-37
1. Where did Maniac go? What did he do? What did he eat?
2. What happened whenever he crossed the bridge over the Schuylkill River?
3. What did Maniac do at Valley Forge?
4. Whom did Maniac meet at Valley Forge? What did he convince them to do? What did he discover about them?
5. Describe the McNab house.
6. Russell and Piper told Maniac they were getting ready to shoot at the enemy. Who was the enemy?
7. What deals did Maniac make with Russell and Piper? Did it work? Why or why not?
8. What were some of Maniac's heroic feats?
9. How did Maniac feel about these feats?
10. What was the most perilous challenge?

Chapters 38-41
1. Describe the race. Who was in it? Who won? How did the winner feel? How did the loser feel?
2. Where did Maniac go after the race? What happened there?
3. What were the McNabs building, and why?
4. Where did Maniac go that night?
5. Why did he leave the McNabs' house?
6. Maniac went back for Piper's birthday party, and took a guest. Who was the guest? Why did Maniac bring him?
7. Describe dinner at the Pickwell house that same night. Who were the extra guests? How did the family react?
8. What did one of the guests do when the two of them got ready to cross Marshall Street?
9. How did Maniac's guest feel when they got to the party?

Chapters 42-46
1. What present did Maniac take for Piper, and under what conditions could he have it?
2. What was George McNab's reaction to the guest?
3. One of the Cobras jumped through the hole from the second floor to the first. What happened after he jumped?
4. What miracle had happened while the boys were at the party?
6. Who started running with Maniac? Describe the way they ran.
7. Describe the meeting with Piper and Russell.
8. Two days later, Mars Bar visited Maniac and asked him why he didn't try to rescue Russell. What was Maniac's answer? What was Mars Bar's reaction?
9. What happened to Russell?
10. What did Mars Bar invite Maniac to do? What was Maniac's answer?
11. How did the story end?
12. How did Maniac feel at the end of the book?

ANSWER KEY: SHORT ANSWER STUDY QUESTIONS *Maniac Magee*

Chapters 1-5

1. What was Maniac's real name?
    It was Jeffrey Lionel Magee.

2. With whom did Maniac live, and why? What was his life there like? How long did he live that way?
    Maniac lived with his Aunt Dot and Uncle Dan. When he was three, his parents were killed when the trolley they were on crashed into the river. His aunt and uncle did not speak to each other. They had two of everything. Maniac spent part of his time with each one of them. He lived like that for eight years.

3. What happened the night of the musical?
    Maniac was in the chorus. When the singing stopped, he was still screaming "Talk! Talk, will ya!" He ran down from the risers and kept on going.

4. Where did he go when he left Hollidaysburg? How long did it take him to get there?
    He went to Two Mills, across the river from Bridgeport. It took him a year to get there.

5. What did people see and hear when they saw Maniac on his first day in town?
    They saw a scraggly little kid. The soles of his sneakers were falling off. He said "Hi" as he passed each of them.

6. Who was the first person Maniac talked with? Describe their meeting.
    She was Amanda Beale. She was on her way to school, and was carrying a suitcase full of books. Maniac asked if he could borrow one. Amanda was surprised to see a white boy in the East End. After they ran and talked for a while, she agreed to give him a book. It was one on the Children's Crusade.

7. Who lived in the East End? Who lived in the West End?
    The blacks lived in the East End, and the whites lived in the West End.

8. Describe Maniac's meeting with Brian Denehy and James "Hands" Down.
    The eleventh grade gym class was in session on the high school field. Brian Denehy, the star quarterback, threw a pass to James "Hands" Down. Maniac intercepted the pass, punted the ball, and it landed in the hands of Hands Down. Maniac did all but the punt with one hand, because he had Amanda's book in the other one. Everyone was surprised.

9. Describe what happened at Finsterwald's house.
> The young kids were afraid to go near Finsterwald's house. A group of high school kids dumped Arnold Jones into Finsterwald's back yard and ran off. Arnold got the "finsterwallies", or violent shakes. Then the high school kids saw Maniac go into the yard (accounts differed on whether he jumped the fence or opened the gate). Arnold fainted. Maniac picked him up and carried him to the front step. Arnold woke up and ran away. Maniac sat on the steps and started reading.

Chapters 6-11

1. Describe dinner at the Pickwell home. How did the children know it was time for dinner? How many family members ate there?
> Mrs. Pickwell blew a whistle and all of the kids ran home. There were 18 Pickewells in all: ten children, the parents, the baby, Grandmother, Grandfather, Great-grandfather, a taxi driver, and Jeffrey.

2. After dinner, Jeffrey ran somewhere. Where did he run? Why were the Pickwell kids surprised?
> Jeffrey ran on the railroad tracks with a book in his hand. This surprised the Pickwell kids, because the other kids had only walked on the track. No one had been able to run on the steel rail.

3. Describe John McNab. Why wasn't the rest of the league any match for him?
> John McNab was a giant compared to the rest of the Little League players. He was 5'8" tall and weighed more than 170 pounds. People didn't believe he was only twelve. He was a pitcher, and threw a fastball that most of the other players could not hit.

4. Describe the play between Jeffrey as batter and John McNab as pitcher.
> McNab pitched his fastball. Jeffrey hit it, and the ball nipped McNab's cap, landed near second base, and rolled to the fence in center field. McNab pitched again and Jeffrey poled it. The next ball cleared the fence. Then Jeffrey got three home runs. McNab took a time out to relieve himself. When he came back, he threw a frog at Jeffrey instead of a ball. Jeffrey bunted the frog and took off to get an inside-the-park-home-run-bunt. The frog started hopping down the third base line, McNab tried to herd it across the line for a foul, but the frog changed directions. Jeffrey crossed home plate, grabbed his book, and started running while the audience cheered. McNab told him never to come back.

5. How did Jeffrey get the name "Maniac"?
> The people in the town were all talking about him and his deeds. Someone probably said, "Kid's gotta be a maniac." Others agreed. Since they didn't know his real name, they started calling him Maniac.

6. Where did Jeffrey sleep?
   He slept in the deer shed at the Elmwood Park Zoo.

7. How did he like Amanda's book?
   He was so fascinated that he read it over and over.

8. What did John McNab try to do to get even? What happened?
   McNab and his pals, the Cobras, found Maniac running on the train rail. They started throwing stones at him. Maniac started heading for the Pickwell house. After a while he noticed that the kids behind him were laughing. They were standing at Hector Street. Hector Street was the boundary between the black East End and the white West End. The Cobras figured Maniac would have trouble if he went into the East End.

9. What unthinkable thing did Maniac do when he met Mars Bar Thompson? Why was it so unthinkable?
   He took a bite of the candy Mars Bar offered him. Maniac bit right over the spot where Mars Bar had eaten. It was unthinkable because Mars Bar was black and Maniac was white.

10. Describe the scene with Maniac's book.
    Mars Bar snatched the book. Maniac snatched it back, but Mars Bar held on, and one page ripped. Maniac was trying to take it back when a woman stopped them and made Mars Bar return the page.

11. What happened while Maniac was trying to find Amanda's house?
    Mars Bar and some friends followed him and backed him against a wall. Amanda found them. She saw the damage to her book, knew Mars Bar had caused it, and began kicking him. He ran away. She invited Manic to her house and he accepted.

Chapters 12-16

1. How did Maniac end up staying with the Beale family?
   Mr. Beale offered to drive him home. Maniac told Mr. Beale to stop the car at a house that was in the black neighborhood. When Mr. Beale pointed this out, Maniac told him the whole story. Mr. Beale brought Maniac back to the Beale house, and Mrs. Beale agreed that he should stay.

2. What was "the miracle on Sycamore Street"?
   Maniac did jobs around the house, played with Hester and Lester, turned out lights, and kept his room neat.

3. Describe some of the other changes in the Beale household.
    Hester and Lester stopped crayoning on the walls and furniture. Mrs. Beale had time to relax. Hester and Lester began taking baths willingly, because Maniac got in the tub with them. The little ones stopped damaging Amanda's books.

4. What was Maniac's allergy?
    He was allergic to pizza.

5. How did Maniac feel about his new life?
    He loved it.

6. How did the West End kids find out Jeffrey was "that Maniac kid?"
    Jeffrey was playing football with Hands Down. The other kids noticed the way he ran. They also noticed the way he poled the ball when they played stickball. They started thinking about the rumors about the Maniac kid, and figured out that Jeffrey was the Maniac.

7. What was Jeffrey afraid of losing, and why?
    He was afraid of losing his name, the only thing he had left from his parents.

8. How did the kids in the East End react to Maniac?
    The preschoolers came to him to untie their sneaker knots. The bigger kids tested his sports ability. Hands Down talked for him.

9. How was Maniac blind?
    He didn't see that big kids didn't like little ones showing them up. He didn't see that the big kids didn't like having another big kid (Hands Down) laughing at them while the little one showed them up. He didn't see that some kids didn't like him because he was different, especially a different color.

10. What did Manic think about skin color?
    He couldn't understand it. He didn't think he was white: he was a combination of different shades and colors.

Chapters 17-21

1. What happened to Maniac while the children were playing in the fire hydrant water?
    An old black man called him "Whitey" and told him to go back to his own kind.

2. What was on the wall of the Beales' house a few days later? How did the family react? How did Maniac react?

It was the words Fishbelly Go Home in chalk. The children tried to distract him from coming home from his run so that Mrs. Beale could scrub it off. After he saw it, he said he would leave and go live at the zoo.

3. Amanda and Maniac had an argument. What did Amanda say that she felt sorry for?
   She told Jeffrey that if he left their house he would not be able to get a library card, because he would not have an address.

4. Describe Cobble's Knot. Where was it? What was the prize for untying it?
   It was a large ball of string that no one had been able to untangle. Mr. Cobble kept it in a secret place inside his store, Cobble's Corner Grocery. The prize for untying it was one large pizza a week for a year.

5. Why did Amanda want Maniac to untie the knot?
   If he untied it, he would get his picture in the paper and be a big hero. She thought it would help him be accepted in the neighborhood.

6. Did Maniac untie the knot?
   Yes, he did.

7. What did Maniac and Amanda discover about the confetti? What did Maniac do?
   They discovered that someone had gone into the Beale's living room, taken the Encyclopedia A, and ripped it up for confetti. When Maniac saw it, he started walking out of town.

8. Describe the way Maniac walked out of town.
   He walked down the middle of Hector Street. McNab and the Cobras were on the west curb, and Mars Bar and his friends were on the east curb. Both sides were calling for him to come over. Then they started yelling and cursing at each other. No one stepped off a curb. Maniac walked out of town.

Chapters 22-26

1. Where was Maniac living?
   He was living in the buffalo pen at the Elmwood Park Zoo.

2. Who found Maniac? Where did they go? What did they do?
   Grayson, the park attendant, found Maniac lying on the ground outside the pen. He took Maniac to the baseball equipment room in the empty band shell. Grayson got some food for Maniac, and then Maniac told him his story. Then Maniac went with Grayson in the truck to get some Butterscotch Krimpets.

3. What did they do after Grayson bought the Krimpets?
   Grayson took Maniac to his home at the Two Mills YMCA, and got him a shower. Then he took Maniac shopping and bought him some clothes.

4. Where did Maniac say he wanted to stay?
   He said he wanted to stay in the locker room at the band shell.

5. Grayson asked Maniac about school. What was Maniac's answer?
   He said he did not want to go to school. He did not tell Grayson why, but he thought that he did not want to have school if he did not have a home. He told Grayson he would run away if Grayson tried to make him go to school.

6. What kind of questions did Grayson ask Maniac?
   He asked questions about the way the black people in the East End lived. He wanted to know what they ate, if they brushed their teeth, and if they drank out of the same glass in the bathroom.

7. What did Grayson invite Maniac to do, and what was Maniac's reply?
   Grayson invited Maniac to stay with him at the YMCA, but Maniac said he wanted to stay at the band shell.

8. What did Maniac discover about Grayson's past?
   Grayson had been a minor league baseball player.

9. How did Maniac and Grayson begin spending their afternoons?
   Maniac would go with Grayson and help him repair fences around the park. Grayson told baseball stories and fed Maniac. Grayson began giving Maniac instructions on how to play baseball.

10. How was Maniac keeping up with his education?
    He used the money Grayson gave him for Krimpets, and bought used books at the library. Every morning he read and studied.

11. What did Grayson ask Maniac to do?
    Grayson asked Maniac to teach him to read.

Chapters 27-32

1. Maniac taught Grayson to read. When did they work? What kind of books did he use? What was difficult, and what was easy for Grayson?

    Grayson took the mornings off to study. They bought children's books at the library book sale. They bought a small blackboard and chalk at Woolworth's. Grayson learned the alphabet in three days. He read ten one-syllable words the first week. In a few more weeks he could sound out new words. The consonants were easy, but the vowels were difficult.

2. What was the first book Grayson read? How did Maniac react?

    The book was *The Little Engine That Could.* Maniac said, "A-men." Then they hugged. Maniac served corn muffins and apple juice. Maniac invited Grayson to spend the night, and he did.

3. How was the room different than when Maniac first moved in?

    It had some furniture, a toaster oven, a space heater, dishes, and was looking homey.

4. How did Maniac and Grayson spend Thanksgiving?

    They went to the high school football game. After that, they cooked a chicken in Maniac's toaster oven. Maniac said a prayer. Then they listened and danced to Grayson's polka records.

5. What did Maniac do with the paint?

    He used brown paint to put the numerals 101 on the outside of the door.

6. What did they do at Christmas? Where was Grayson living?

    Grayson had moved in with Maniac. They decorated the room, and put up a tree. They also trimmed a tree in the woods.

7. What did they do on Christmas Day? What presents did they give each other?

    In the morning, they visited their decorated tree in the woods. Then they visited the animals in the zoo. Maniac gave the baby buffalo a scarf. Maniac gave Grayson a pair of gloves, a scarf, and a book. The book was titled *The Man Who Struck Out Willie Mays*, by Jeffrey L. Magee. Grayson gave Maniac a box of Butterscotch Krimpets, a new baseball, and his own glove.

8. What did Maniac do when he discovered Grayson was dead?

    He held Grayson's hand and talked to him. He read aloud all the books Grayson had read. That night, he put his chest protectors next to Grayson's cot, lay down, and cried. The next day he told the zookeeper.

9. Describe the funeral.
> Maniac was the only person there besides the pallbearers and the man from the funeral home. He ran away before the minister got there.

Chapters 33-37

1. Where did Maniac go? What did he do? What did he eat?
> He took a few things from the band shell and painted over the numerals. He ran all over the area. At night he slept at the zoo, in abandoned cars, garages, or stairwells. He ate at the zoo or in soup kitchens.

2. What happened whenever he crossed the bridge over the Schuylkill River?
> He turned his eyes away from the P&W trestle. He still thought about his parents being killed when the train went into the water.

3. What did Maniac do at Valley Forge?
> He stayed in one of the old Revolutionary War cabins. He was waiting for death.

4. Whom did Maniac meet at Valley Forge? What did he convince them to do? What did he discover about them?
> He met two little boys, Piper and Russell. They were brothers who were running away to Mexico. Maniac convinced them to go home by offering them a free pizza and telling them he would tell them a short cut to Mexico on the next day. When they got near Cobble's he found out that their older brother was John McNab.

5. Describe the McNab house.
> It was smelly and dirty. The dog had relieved itself on the floor. There were cans, bottles, and garbage all over. There was a partially dissected bird on the kitchen table. The only foods in the refrigerator were beer and mustard.

6. Russell and Piper told Maniac they were getting ready to shoot at the enemy. Who was the enemy?
> The enemy was the black people in the East End.

7. What deals did Maniac make with Russell and Piper? Did it work? Why or why not?
> The first week, he told them he would show them the way to Mexico on Saturday if they would go to school all week. The next week he offered them a pizza if they went to school for that week. The little kids started asking them to have Maniac undo sneaker knots. The boys began feeling important. The next week they asked Maniac to stay in Finsterwald's yard for ten minutes. Maniac did, then offered to knock on the front door. He did, and the boys went to school for two more weeks.

8. What were some of Maniac's heroic feats?
   He hit a telephone pole with a stone 61 times in a row. He ran on one rail and beat the train. He stuck his hand and arm into a mysterious hole. He climbed the fence at the bison pen and kissed the baby buffalo.

9. How did Maniac feel about these feats?
   He understood that he was doing them to keep the McNab boys in school. He also enjoyed meeting their challenges.

10. What was the most perilous challenge?
    They dared him to go into the East End.

Chapters 38-41

1. Describe the race. Who was in it? Who won? How did the winner feel? How did the loser feel?
   Mars Bar greeted Maniac when he was about four blocks into the East End. He showed Maniac his new sneakers and challenged him to a race. Maniac won the race. He turned around at the last minute to look at Mars Bar, and won the race going backwards. The crowd went wild. Maniac was upset. He was not sure why he did it. Mars Bar complained that Maniac had cheated, and that the kids holding the thread had moved it.

2. Where did Maniac go after the race? What happened there?
   He went to the Beales' house. They were all glad to see him. He spent the night and left early the next morning.

3. What were the McNabs building, and why?
   They were building a pillbox. They thought the blacks in the East End were going to revolt, and they wanted to be ready for it.

4. Where did Maniac go that night?
   He went to the Pickwell house for dinner.

5. Why did he leave the McNabs' house?
   He did not have any influence left over the boys. They told him to leave, and he did.

6. Maniac went back for Piper's birthday party, and took a guest. Who was the guest? Why did Maniac bring him?
   The guest was Mars Bar Thompson. Maniac thought it was a good idea because the blacks and the whites did not know much about each other.

7. Describe dinner at the Pickwell house that same night. Who were the extra guests? How did the family react?

Maniac and Mars Bar had dinner at the Pickwell house before they went to the party. They were welcomed. Mars Bar was pleased to find out that he was famous in the West End.

8. What did one of the guests do when the two of them got ready to cross Marshall Street?
   When they came to Marshall Street, Mars Bar did his famous shuffle. He stood in the middle of the street and glared at everyone for a minute.

9. How did Maniac's guest feel when they got to the party?
   He was uneasy.

Chapters 42-46

1. What present did Maniac take for Piper, and under what conditions could he have it?
   He took a compass. He told Piper he could have the compass if both boys went to school every day until the school year was finished.

2. What was George McNab's reaction to the guest?
   He went upstairs and told the others to let him know when Mars Bar left. He referred to Mars Bar as "it."

3. What happened after one of the Cobras jumped through the hole from the second floor?
   He landed behind Mars Bar. Mars Bar wanted to charge the boy, but Maniac held him back. John McNab and Mars Bar traded insults. Maniac dragged Mars Bar out.

4. What miracle had happened while the boys were at the party?
   Maniac realized he was proud of Mars Bar for not showing his fear.

5. Where did Maniac stay at night, now that he was not staying at the McNab house? What did he do during the day?
   He slept in the park, in the buffalo shed, the band shell. He started staying in a different backyard each night. During the day he read in the library or played in the park. He often went to the Pickwell house for dinner.

6. Who started running with Maniac? Describe the way they ran.
   Mars Bar began running. They met in alleys or intersections. They started running the same route for a block or two, and increased the time they ran together. They pretended not to see each other, but kept their pace the same.

7. Describe the meeting with Piper and Russell.
   Russell was stuck out on the trolley trestle over the river. There was a trolley about twenty feet from him. Piper asked Maniac and Mars Bar to save Russell. Maniac left the platform and walked away.

8. Two days later, Mars Bar visited Maniac and asked him why he didn't try to rescue Russell. What was Maniac's answer? What was Mars Bar's reaction?
   He told Mars Bar the story of his parents' death. Mars Bar said he knew Maniac was not scared.

9. What happened to Russell?
   Mars Bar rescued him and took both boys to his home. His mother dried them off and they stayed and played for the day. Mr. Thompson took them home that night.

10. What did Mars Bar invite Maniac to do? What was Maniac's answer?
    Mars Bar invited Maniac to stay at his home for a while. Maniac said he couldn't. Then he ran away.

11. How did the story end?
    Mars Bar woke Amanda and took her with him to the buffalo pen. She woke Maniac and told him he was coming home with her. He tried to refuse, but she insisted.

12. How did Maniac feel at the end of the book?
    He was content. He knew he was really going home.

MULTIPLE CHOICE STUDY/QUIZ QUESTIONS *Maniac Magee*

Chapters 1-5
1. What was Maniac's real name?
   A. It was Jeffrey Lytel McGee.
   B. It was John Lionel Macintosh.
   C. It was Jeffrey Lionel Magee.
   D. It was Joshua Little McGinty.

2. Which of the following does **not** describe Maniac's early life?
   A. Maniac lived with his older sister and her husband.
   B. When he was three, his parents were killed when the trolley they were on crashed into the river.
   C. His relatives did not speak to each other. They had two of everything. Maniac spent part of his time with each one of them.
   D. He lived with them for eight years.

3. True or False: After the musical, Maniac was screaming. He ran down from the risers and kept on going.
   A. True
   B. False

4. Where did he go when he left Hollidaysburg? How long did it take him to get there?
   A. He went to Three Rivers, near Norristown. It took him a week to get there.
   B. He went to Jeffersonville. It took him six months to get there.
   C. He went to Five Points, near Schuylkill. It took him two days to get there.
   D. He went to Two Mills, near Bridgeport. It took him a year to get there.

5. True or False: Maniac was well dressed, and was wearing new sneakers.
   A. True
   B. False

6. Who was Amanda Beale?
   A. She was a teacher Maniac met when he went to enroll in school.
   B. She was the town librarian.
   C. She was a student, about Maniac's age, who was on her way to school.
   D. She was a social worker.

Maniac Magee Multiple Choice Questions

7. What did Maniac borrow?
    A. He borrowed a book on the Children's Crusade.
    B. He borrowed money for breakfast.
    C. He borrowed a jacket.
    D. He borrowed pencils, paper, and crayons to use in school.

8. Which statement is **true**?
    A. The blacks lived in North Mills and the whites lived in South Mills.
    B. The blacks lived in Westport and the whites lived in Eastport.
    C. The blacks lived in the South Side and the whites lived in the North Side.
    D. The blacks lived in the East End, and the whites lived in the West End.

9. Describe Maniac's meeting with Brian Denehy and James "Hands" Down.
    A. They were playing basketball. Maniac took the ball away from James "Hands" Down and scored a three point goal.
    B. They were playing football. Maniac intercepted a pass, from Brian Denehy, punted the ball, and it landed in the hands of Hands Down.
    C. They were playing baseball. Hands Down was pitching to Brian Denehy. Maniac caught the ball and caused Brian's team to lose the game.
    D. Brian and James "Hands" Down were the stars of the track team. Maniac ran faster than both of them during a practice.

10. A group of high school kids dumped Arnold Jones into Finsterwald's back yard and ran off. Arnold got the "finsterwallies", or violent shakes. What did Maniac do?
    A. He threw two of the high school boys over the fence and made them bring Arnold out.
    B. He rang Finsterwald's doorbell and asked if he could have the key to unlock the gate.
    C. Maniac carried Arnold to the front step. Then Maniac sat on the steps and started reading.
    D. Maniac helped Arnold climb over the back fence. Then the two of them went to the drugstore for sodas.

Maniac Magee Multiple Choice Questions

Chapters 6-11
1. Which of the following statements does **not** describe dinner at the Pickwell home?
    A. There were ten Pickwell children.
    B. Mrs. Pickwell rang a big dinner bell and all of the kids ran home.
    C. None of the kids were ever late for dinner.
    D. Mr. Pickwell also invited a taxi driver for dinner.

2. After dinner, Jeffrey ran somewhere that the other kids had only walked. Where was it?
    A. Jeffrey ran up the side of the mountain in his bare feet.
    B. Jeffrey ran along the roofs of the houses on Hector Street.
    C. Jeffrey ran the entire length of the P&W trolley route in one hour.
    D. Jeffrey ran on the railroad tracks with a book in his hand.

3. Which sentence describes John McNab?
    A. John McNab was 14 years old, 6' 5" tall, and weighed 210 pounds. He threw a spinball that no one could hit.
    B. John McNab was 12 years old, 5' 8" tall, and weighed more than 170 pounds. He threw a fastball that most of the other players could not hit.
    C. John McNab was 13 years old. He was only 4' 9" tall, and weighed 100 pounds. He could run bases faster than anyone else in the league.
    D. John McNab was 11 years old. He was 5' 5" tall. He had powerful arms and could hit a home run farther than anyone else.

4. How did the play between Jeffrey and John McNab end?
    A. McNab pitched a frog. Jeffrey bunted it and made a home run.
    B. McNab pitched a fast ball. Jeffrey hit it out of the park, ran after it, and never came back.
    C. Jeffrey pitched his famous Maniac ball. McNab could not hit it, and lost the game.
    D. Jeffrey pitched a slow ball. McNab hit it, but Maniac caught it in the air and tagged him out.

5. True or False: The people in the town were all taking about Jeffrey and his deeds. Someone probably said, "Kid's gotta be a maniac." Others agreed. Since they didn't know his real name, they started calling him Maniac.
    A. True
    B. False

Maniac Magee Multiple Choice Questions

6. Where did Jeffrey sleep?
    A. He slept in a junkyard full of abandoned cars.
    B. He slept in the basement storeroom of the library. He sneaked in through a broken window.
    C. He slept in the deer shed at the Elmwood Park Zoo.
    D. He slept in the garage at one of the churches in town.

7. How did he like Amanda's book?
    A. He didn't like it, but did not remember where she lived to take it back.
    B. He liked the pictures, but could not read the words.
    C. He liked it but was bored after he read it once.
    D. He was so fascinated that he read it over and over.

8. McNab and his pals, the Cobras, found Maniac running on the train rail. They started throwing stones at him. Where did Maniac run to get away from them?
    A. He ran into the Pickwell house.
    B. He ran to the buffalo pen at the zoo.
    C. He ran across Hector Street into the East End.
    D. He ran up the P&W trestle and ran on the bridge over the river.

9. True or False: Maniac challenged Mars Bar to a race through the neighborhood. It was unthinkable because no white boy had ever run through the black neighborhood.
    A. True
    B. False

10. What happened to Amanda's book when Mars Bar snatched it?
    A. Mars Bar set it on fire.
    B. Maniac got it back and it was in perfect condition.
    C. Mars Bar threw it in the street and a truck ran over it.
    D. One page ripped before Maniac got it back.

11. Mars Bar and some friends followed Maniac and backed him against a wall. What happened **next**?
    A. A woman in the neighborhood hit Mars Bar and the others with her broom and chased them away.
    B. A policeman saw them and stopped the fight.
    C. Amanda found them. She kicked Mars Bar, Then she invited Manic to her house.
    D. Maniac jumped over the wall and ran away.

Maniac Magee Multiple Choice Questions

Chapters 12-16

1. What happened when Maniac told Mr. Beale the true story about where he lived?
    A. Mr. Beale drove Maniac to the zoo.
    B. Mr. Beale took him to the police station and asked the officers to take care of him.
    C. Mr. Beale said he would have to call Social Services the next day.
    D. Mr. Beale took him back to the Beale home. Mrs. Beale agreed that he should stay.

2. Maniac did jobs around the house, played with Hester and Lester, turned out lights, and kept his room neat. What did Mrs. Beale call this?
    A. She called it "the Maniac Phenomenon."
    B. She called it "the miracle on Sycamore Street."
    C. She called it "Beale's Best Guest."
    D. She called it " Extraordinary East End Excellence"

3. Which of the following did **not** happen in the Beale household?
    A. Hester and Lester started eating vegetables for dinner every night.
    B. Hester and Lester stopped crayoning on the walls and furniture.
    C. Hester and Lester began taking baths willingly.
    D. Hester and Lester stopped damaging Amanda's books.

4. What was Maniac's allergy?
    A. He was allergic to milk.
    B. He was allergic to his feather pillow.
    C. He was allergic to pizza.
    D. He was allergic to the bubble bath Mrs. Beale used.

5. True or False: Maniac liked his new life, but wished he could go back to his old life.
    A. True
    B. False

6. True or False: The East End kids figured out that Jeffrey was the Maniac kid because of the way he played football, stickball, and other sports.
    A. True
    B. False

Maniac Magee Multiple Choice Questions

7. What was Jeffrey afraid of losing?
    A. He was afraid of losing the Beale family and his home, because he was white.
    B. He was afraid of losing Amanda, who was his only friend.
    C. He was afraid of losing his name, the only thing he had left from his parents.
    D. He was afraid of losing his freedom by staying with the Beale family.

8. Which statement about the people in the East End is **false**?
    A. The preschoolers came to him to untie their sneaker knots.
    B. The girls his age thought he was cute.
    C. The bigger kids tested his sports ability.
    D. Hands Down talked for him.

9. True or False: Maniac didn't know that some kids didn't like him.
    A. True
    B. False

10. True or False: Maniac thought he was pure white and his friends in the East End were pure black.
    A. True
    B. False

Maniac Magee Multiple Choice Questions

Chapters 17-21
1. What happened to Maniac while the children were playing in the fire hydrant water?
    A. One of the older boys tried to drown Maniac.
    B. The police stopped and asked him what he was doing in the East End.
    C. He slipped and broke his leg.
    D. An old man called him "Whitey" and told him to go back to his own kind.

2. What was on the wall of the Beales' house a few days later?
    A. It was the words *Go Away Maniac*.
    B. It was a picture of Maniac with an "X" across it.
    C. It was the words *Fishbelly Go Home* in chalk.
    D. It was the words *Beales Love Whitey*.

3. Amanda and Maniac had an argument. What did Amanda say that she felt sorry for afterwards?
    A. She told Jeffrey that if he left their house he would not be able to get a library card, because he would not have an address.
    B. She told Jeffrey he would never be a real member of her family anyway, so he might as well leave.
    C. She told Jeffrey they were only letting him stay because the was a free babysitter for the little kids.
    D. She told Jeffrey he would never find a real home because he was a maniac.

4. Describe Cobble's Knot.
    A. It was a sneaker lace that had knots from one end to the other.
    B. It was a large ball of string that no one had been able to untangle.
    C. It was a necktie that had lot of knots in it.
    D. It was a rope full of square knots. A Boy Scout troop had made it.

5. What was the prize for untying Cobble's Knot?
    A. The prize for untying it was a free pass to the movie theater for a month.
    B. The prize for untying it was one hundred dollars.
    C. The prize for untying it was one large pizza a week for a year.
    D. The prize for untying it was a fifteen minute shopping spree in Cobble's Store.

6. True or False: Amanda wanted Maniac give the prize to her parents.
    A. True
    B. False

Maniac Magee Multiple Choice Questions

7. Did Maniac untie the knot?
    A. No, he did not.
    B. Yes, he did.

8. True or False: The confetti was made from ripped pages from Amanda's Encyclopedia.
    A. True
    B. False

9. True or False: Maniac thought the right thing for him to do was to get whoever made the confetti.
    A. True
    B. False

10. Describe the way Maniac left town.
    A. He ran on the P&W track.
    B. Mr. Beale drove him.
    C. He rode Amanda's bicycle.
    D. He walked down the middle of Hector Street.

Maniac Magee Multiple Choice Questions

<u>Chapters 22-26</u>
1. Where was Maniac living?
    A. He was living at a homeless shelter in downtown Bridgeport.
    B. He was living in a cardboard box behind the shopping center.
    C. He was living in the buffalo pen at the Elmwood Park Zoo.
    D. He was living in a hollow tree in the woods.

2. Grayson found Maniac. Where did he take Maniac?
    A. He took Maniac to the school principal.
    B. He took Maniac to the emergency room at the hospital.
    C. He took Maniac to the empty band shell.
    D. He took Maniac to his daughter's house.

3. What did Grayson and Maniac do **first**?
    A. They went shopping for new clothes for Maniac.
    B. They went to the YMCA and Maniac had a shower.
    C. They drove around the park.
    D. They went out to buy Butterscotch Krimpets.

4. True or False: Grayson was the park superintendent.
    A. True
    B. False

5. True or False: Maniac said he would run away if Grayson tried to make him go to school.
    A. True
    B. False

6. What kind of questions did Grayson ask Maniac?
    A. He asked questions about Maniac's life before he came to Two Mills.
    B. He asked questions about the way the black people in the East End lived.
    C. He wanted to know Maniac's favorite foods.
    D. He wanted to know how Maniac untied Cobble's Knot.

7. True or False: Maniac said he wanted to stay at the YMCA with Grayson.
    A. True
    B. False

Maniac Magee Multiple Choice Questions

8. What did Maniac discover about Grayson's past?
    A. Grayson had been in jail for robbery.
    B. Grayson had been a hero in World War II.
    C. Grayson had been a minor league baseball player.
    D. Grayson's wife and children had been killed in a train wreck.

9. What did Maniac and Grayson do together in the afternoons?
    A. They ran track, cleaned the zoo, and cooked dinner.
    B. They drove around town and collected tin cans to recycle.
    C. They fed the animals at the zoo and watched TV at the YMCA.
    D. They repaired fences, told stories, and played baseball.

10. How was Maniac keeping up with his education?
    A. He was watching educational shows on the television at the department store.
    B. He took old newspapers out of the trash and read them every day.
    C. He read books at the bookstore in town.
    D. He used the money Grayson gave him for Krimpets, and bought used books at the library. Every morning he read and studied.

11. What did Grayson ask Maniac to do?
    A. Grayson asked Maniac to teach him to read.
    B. Grayson asked Maniac to play baseball with him.
    C. Grayson asked Maniac to call his aunt and uncle and tell them he was fine.
    D. Grayson asked Maniac to call him Grandpa.

Extra Credit: Make a list of major and minor league baseball teams.

MAJOR LEAGUE TEAMS	MINOR LEAGUE TEAMS

Maniac Magee Multiple Choice Questions

Chapters 27-32
1. Maniac taught Grayson to read. What reading material did they use?
    A. They used the sports section of the newspaper.
    B. Maniac wrote stories and Grayson read them.
    C. They used children's books from the library.
    D. They used the street and store signs around town.

2. True or False: The vowels were easy to learn.
    A. True
    B. False

3. What was the first book Grayson read?
    A. The book was *Mike Mulligan and His Steam Shovel*.
    B. The book was *The Story of Babar*.
    C. The book was *Brown Bear, Brown Bear*.
    D. The book was *The Little Engine That Could*.

4. How did Maniac react when Grayson read his first book?
    A. He jumped up and down and said "Yippee!"
    B. He drew a gold star and pinned it on Grayson's shirt.
    C. He said, "A-men."
    D. He whistled and clapped.

5. Which of these was **not** in Maniac's room?
    A. furniture
    B. a television
    C. a toaster oven
    D. a space heater

6. True or False: Maniac and Grayson had Thanksgiving dinner at the YMCA with some of Grayson's friends.
    A. True
    B. False

Maniac Magee Multiple Choice Questions

7. What did Maniac do with the paint?
    A. He painted the numerals 101 on the outside of the door.
    B. He painted the walls and the floor.
    C. He painted Grayson and Magee on the outside of the door.
    D. He painted the furniture.

8. Where was Grayson living at Christmas time?
    A. He was living in the back of his pick up truck.
    B. He was living in the deer pen at the zoo.
    C. He was still at the YMCA.
    D. He was living in the band shell with Maniac.

9. True or False: Grayson and Maniac put a Christmas tree in the buffalo pen at the zoo.
    A. True
    B. False

10. What did they do on Christmas day?
    A. They watched a parade in Two Mills and ate at a restaurant.
    B. They spent the day in a church to keep warm.
    C. They visited the animals in the zoo. Maniac gave the baby buffalo a scarf.
    D. They went to a party at soup kitchen.

11. True or False: Grayson gave Maniac his own old baseball glove.
    A. True
    B. False

12. What was the name of the book Maniac gave Grayson?
    A. It was *The Little Engine That Could*.
    B. It was *The Adventures of Grayson the Great*.
    C. It was *A History of Baseball*.
    D. It was *The Man Who Struck Out Willie Mays*.

13. What did Maniac do when he discovered Grayson was dead?
    A. He told the zookeeper right away.
    B. He ran out of the room and locked it. He stayed outside for two days.
    C. He held Grayson's hand, talked to him and read aloud all his books.
    D. He cried and screamed. He shook Grayson and yelled. "Wake up."

14. True or False: Maniac ran away from the funeral before the minister got there.
    A. True
    B. False

Extra Credit: What would Maniac put in the book he wrote for Grayson? Draw a picture and write a few sentences on the book page below.

Maniac Magee Multiple Choice Questions

Chapters 33-37
1. True or False: After Grayson died, Maniac moved into his old room at the YMCA.
    A. True
    B. False

2. When did Maniac think about his parents being killed?
    A. He thought about it every time he visited Grayson's tomb at the cemetery.
    B. He thought about it every night before he went to sleep.
    C. He thought about it whenever he took a bath in the lake in the park.
    D. He thought about it whenever he crossed the bridge over the Schuylkill River.

3. What was Maniac doing at Valley Forge?
    A. He was waiting for death.
    B. He was studying the history of the Revolutionary War.
    C. He was hiding from the Cobras.
    D. He was looking for leftover food from tourists.

4. True or False: The two little boys were John Mc Nab's brothers.
    A. True
    B. False

5. True or False: The McNab house was neat and clean.
    A. True
    B. False

6. Russell and Piper were getting ready to shoot at the enemy. Who was the enemy?
    A. The enemy was the Social Services worker.
    B. The enemy was the police.
    C. The enemy was the black people in the East End.
    D. The enemy was the Cobras.

7. Maniac made deals with Russell and Piper. Why did they work?
    A. Maniac gave them a lot of money and food.
    B. They started to like getting good grades in school.
    C. They were afraid of him because of his reputation.
    D. The boys began feeling important.

Maniac Magee Multiple Choice Questions

8. Which is **not** one of Maniac's heroic feats?
    A. He hit a telephone pole with a stone 61 times in a row.
    B. He ran on one rail and beat the train.
    C. He ate a whole box of Butterscotch Krimpets at one time.
    D. He climbed the fence at the bison pen and kissed the baby buffalo.

9. True or False: Maniac enjoyed meeting the challenges of the McNab boys.
    A. True
    B. False

10. True or False: The most perilous challenge was sleeping in Finsterwald's yard overnight.
    A. True
    B. False

Maniac Magee Multiple Choice Questions

Chapters 38-41

1. Who won the race?
    - A. Mars Bar won the race.
    - B. Maniac won the race.

2. Where did Maniac go after the race?
    - A. He went to the library.
    - B. He went to the buffalo pen at the zoo.
    - C. He went to the Beales' house for dinner.
    - D. He kept running on the railroad tracks.

3. True or False: The McNabs were building a pillbox. They thought the blacks in the East End were going to revolt, and they wanted to be ready for it.
    - A. True
    - B. False

4. Where did Maniac go that night?
    - A. He went back to the cabin at Valley Forge to sleep.
    - B. He went to his old room at the band shell.
    - C. He went to Amanda's house.
    - D. He went to the Pickwell house for dinner.

5. True or False: Maniac left the McNabs' house because he did not have any influence left over the boys.
    - A. True
    - B. False

6. Maniac went back for Piper's birthday party, and took a guest. Who was the guest?
    - A. The guest was Amanda Beale.
    - B. The guest was Duke Pickwell.
    - C. The guest was Mars Bar Thompson.
    - D. The guest was the baby bison.

7. Where did Maniac and Mars Bar eat dinner that night?
    - A. They ate at Mars Bar's house.
    - B. They ate at the Pickwell house.
    - C. They ate with Amanda's family.
    - D. They ate at the zoo.

Maniac Magee Multiple Choice Questions

8. True or False: When the boys came to Marshall Street, Maniac did his famous shuffle. He stood in the middle of the street and glared at everyone for a minute.
    A. True
    B. False

9. How did Maniac's guest feel when they got to the party?
    A. He was angry.
    B. He was happy.
    C. He was uneasy.
    D. He was terrified.

Maniac Magee Multiple Choice Questions

Chapters 42-46

1. What present did Maniac take for Piper?
    - A. He took a book.
    - B. He took a toy sub-machine gun.
    - C. He took a compass.
    - D. He took a bag of cookies.

2. True or False: George McNab called Mars Bar "it."
    - A. True
    - B. False

3. One of the Cobras jumped through the hole from the second floor to the first. What happened after he jumped?
    - A. He fell and broke his leg.
    - B. He landed on top of Maniac.
    - C. He fell on the pillbox and broke part of it.
    - D. He landed behind Mars Bar.

4. True or False: Mars Bar said he was glad he went to the party.
    - A. True
    - B. False

5. True or False: Maniac started staying in a different backyard each night.
    - A. True
    - B. False

6. Who started running with Maniac?
    - A. Hester and Lester began running with Maniac.
    - B. Amanda began running with Maniac.
    - C. Russell and Piper began running with Maniac.
    - D. Mars Bar began running with Maniac.

7. Did Maniac save Russell when he was stuck on the trolley trestle?
    - A. Yes, he did.
    - B. No, he did not.

Maniac Magee Multiple Choice Questions

8. True or False: Mars Bat took Russell and Piper home with him.
   A. True
   B. False

9. Who invited Maniac to be a house guest?
   A. Mrs. Pickwell did.
   B. The zookeeper did.
   C. Mars Bar did.
   D. Russell and Piper did.

10. How did the story end?
    A. Maniac went home with John McNab.
    B. Maniac went back to his aunt and uncle.
    C. Maniac went back to the band shell.
    D. Maniac went back to the Beales' house.

11. How did Maniac feel at the end of the book?
    A. He was scared.
    B. He was sad.
    C. He was content.
    D. He was tired.

Extra Credit: Draw a picture of your favorite part of Chapters 42-46. Write a caption for it.

STUDENT ANSWER SHEET-MULTIPLE CHOICE/QUIZ QUESTIONS *Maniac Magee*

Chapters 1-5
1. _____
2. _____
3. _____
4. _____
5. _____
6. _____
7. _____
8. _____
9. _____
10. _____

Chapters 6-11
1. _____
2. _____
3. _____
4. _____
5. _____
6. _____
7. _____
8. _____
9. _____
10. _____
11. _____

Chapters 12-16
1. _____
2. _____
3. _____
4. _____
5. _____
6. _____
7. _____
8. _____
9. _____
10. _____

Chapters 17-21
1. _____
2. _____
3. _____
4. _____
5. _____
6. _____
7. _____
8. _____
9. _____
10. _____

Chapters 22-26
1. _____
2. _____
3. _____
4. _____
5. _____
6. _____
7. _____
8. _____
9. _____
10. _____
11. _____

Chapters 27-32
1. _____
2. _____
3. _____
4. _____
5. _____
6. _____
7. _____
8. _____
9. _____
10. _____
11. _____
12. _____
13. _____
14. _____

Chapters 33-37
1. _____
2. _____
3. _____
4. _____
5. _____
6. _____
7. _____
8. _____
9. _____
10. _____

Chapters 38-41
1. _____
2. _____
3. _____
4. _____
5. _____
6. _____
7. _____
8. _____
9. _____
10. _____

Chapters 42-46
1. _____
2. _____
3. _____
4. _____
5. _____
6. _____
7. _____
8. _____
9. _____
10. _____
11. _____

STUDENT ANSWER SHEET-MULTIPLE CHOICE QUIZ/STUDY QUESTIONS

<u>Chapters 1-5</u>
1. C
2. A
3. A True
4. D
5. B False
6. C
7. A
8. D
9. B
10. C

<u>Chapters 6-11</u>
1. B
2. D
3. B
4. A
5. A True
6. C
7. D
8. C
9. B False
10. D
11. C

<u>Chapters 12-16</u>
1. D
2. B
3. A
4. C
5. B False
6. A True
7. C
8. B
9. A True
10. B False

<u>Chapters 17-21</u>
1. D
2. C
3. A
4. B
5. C
6. B False
7. B
8. A True
9. B False
10. D

<u>Chapters 22-26</u>
1. C
2. C
3. D
4. B False
5. A True
6. B
7. B False
8. C
9. D
10. D
11. A

<u>Chapters 27-32</u>
1. C
2. B False
3. D
4. C
5. B
6. B False
7. A
8. D
9. B False
10. C
11. A True
12. D
13. C
14. A True

<u>Chapters 33-37</u>
1. B False
2. D
3. A
4. A True
5. B False
6. C
7. D
8. C
9. A True
10. B False

<u>Chapters 38-41</u>
1. B
2. C
3. A True
4. D
5. A True
6. C
7. B
8. B False
9. C

<u>Chapters 42-46</u>
1. C
2. A True
3. D
4. B False
5. A True
6. D
7. B
8. A True
9. C
10. D
11. C

PREREADING VOCABULARY WORKSHEETS

Maniac Magee Vocabulary Worksheets

Chapters 1-5
Part I: Using Prior Knowledge and Context Clues
Below are the sentences in which the vocabulary words appear in the text. Read the sentence. Use any clues you can find in the sentence combined with your prior knowledge, and write what you think the underlined words mean on the lines provided.

1. *Maniac* Magee was not born in a dump.

   _____

2. Of course, to be *accurate*, he wasn't really Maniac then. He was Jeffrey Lionel Magee.

   _____

3. Three springy steps down from the risers--girls in pastel dresses screaming, the music director *lunging*--a leap from the stage, out the door and into the starry, sweet, onion-grass- smelling night.

   _____

4. Of course, there's the *obvious* answer that sitting right across the Schuylkill is Bridgeport, where he was born.

   _____

5. Books, all right. Both sides of the suitcase *crammed* with them.

   _____

6. Later on that first day, there was a *commotion* in the West End.

   _____

7. This, of course, was the *infamous* address of Finsterwald.

   _____

8. Suffice it to say that occasionally, even today, if some poor, raggedy, nicotine-stained <u>wretch</u> is seen shuffling through town, word will spread that this once was a bright, happy normal child who had the misfortune of blundering onto Finsterwald's property.

   _____

9. Suffice it to say that occasionally, even today, if some poor, raggedy, nicotine-stained wretch is seen shuffling through town, word will spread that this once was a bright, happy normal child who had the misfortune of <u>*blundering*</u> onto Finsterwald's property.

   _____

10. Arnold Jones was being <u>*hoisted*</u> in the air above Finsterwald's backyard fence.

   _____

Part II: Determining the Meaning Match the vocabulary words to their dictionary definitions.

____ 1.	maniac	A.	apparent; observable
____ 2.	accurate	B.	a person who has extra enthusiasm or desire
____ 3.	lunging	C.	a miserable, unfortunate person
____ 4.	obvious	D.	crowded; packed
____ 5.	crammed	E.	exactly correct
____ 6.	commotion	F.	moving in a clumsy way
____ 7.	infamous	G.	disturbance
____ 8.	wretch	H.	moving forward suddenly
____ 9.	blundering	I.	having a very bad reputation
____ 10.	hoisted	J.	lifted

Maniac Magee Vocabulary Worksheets

Chapters 6-11
Part I: Using Prior Knowledge and Context Clues
Below are the sentences in which the vocabulary words appear in the text. Read the sentence. Use any clues you can find in the sentence combined with your prior knowledge, and write what you think the underlined words mean on the lines provided.

1. They *scanned* the railroad tracks.

   _____

2. McNab froze, then *flinched*, just in time.

   _____

3. *Pandemonium* on the sidelines. It was raining red and green hats.

   _____

4. But now the frog shot through his legs, over to the mound, and now toward shortstop and now toward second, and McNab was *lurching* and lunging, throwing his hat at the frog . . .

   _____

5. Now, as he thought about it, he came to two *conclusions*.

   _____

6. He was at the Oriole Street dead end, but his *instincts* said no, not the street, too much open space.

   _____

7. To old ladies on both sides of Hector Street, it was all but *fatal.*

   _____

8. Judging from that morning, she was pretty *finicky* about her books.

   _____

9. Maniac *cringed* at both prospects.

   _____

10. Suddenly his world was very small and very simple: a brick wall behind him, a row of *scowling* faces in front of him.

    _____

Part II: Determining the Meaning Match the vocabulary words to their dictionary definitions.

____ 1.	scanned	A.	shrunk back in fear
____ 2.	flinched	B.	powerful motivations or impulses
____ 3.	pandemonium	C.	uproar; confusion
____ 4.	lurching	D.	looked over quickly
____ 5.	conclusions	E.	wrinkling the forehead in anger
____ 6.	instincts	F.	deadly
____ 7.	fatal	G.	rolling or pitching suddenly
____ 8.	finicky	H.	choosy; fussy
____ 9.	cringed	I.	winced; recoiled
____ 10.	scowling	J.	end results

Maniac Magee Vocabulary Worksheets

Chapters 12-16
Part I: Using Prior Knowledge and Context Clues
Below are the sentences in which the vocabulary words appear in the text. Read the sentence. Use any clues you can find in the sentence combined with your prior knowledge, and write what you think the underlined words mean on the lines provided.

1. Mr. Beale knew what his passenger *apparently* didn't.

   _____

2. Maniac's lip started to *quiver*, and right there, with the car idling in the middle of the street, Maniac told him that he didn't really have a home, unless you counted the deer shed at the zoo.

   _____

3. Before the puzzled faces of Mr. and Mrs. Beale, he opened the front door and looked at the three cast-iron *digits* nailed to the door frame: seven two eight.

   _____

4. And if their mother wanted to wash their armpits, she would have to get a crowbar and *pry* their arms up, because they sure as heck were not going to move.

   _____

5. So quiet you could hear the water running far below the sewer *grates* while the sun shinnied up the rain spouts.

   _____

6. He loved the silence and *solitude*.

   _____

7. He loved the Fourth of July block party, when the whole East End _converged_ for a day and night of games and music and grilled chicken and ribs and sweet-potato pie and dancing until the last firecracker, and then some.

   _____

8. He loved joining all the colors at the _vacant_ lot and playing the summer days away.

   _____

9. To make matters worse, the supermarket offer had _expired_, so there were no other volumes.

   _____

Part II: Determining the Meaning   Match the vocabulary words to their dictionary definitions.

_____ 1. apparently   A. number symbols
_____ 2. quiver   B. to force open or up
_____ 3. digits   C. aloneness
_____ 4. pry   D. ended
_____ 5. grates   E. to shake with a slight movement
_____ 6. solitude   F. parallel bars for blocking an opening
_____ 7. converged   G. empty
_____ 8. vacant   H. easily understood
_____ 9. expired   I. came together

Maniac Magee Vocabulary Worksheets

Chapters 17-21
Part I: Using Prior Knowledge and Context Clues
Below are the sentences in which the vocabulary words appear in the text. Read the sentence. Use any clues you can find in the sentence combined with your prior knowledge, and write what you think the underlined words mean on the lines provided.

1. Grownups sat on the sidewalk and *dangled* their bare feet in the running gutters.

   _____

2. And the man was croaking, *ranting*, not to Maniac now but to the people.

   _____

3. "I'm *incubating* an egg."

   _____

4. It was made of string, but it had more *contortions*, ins and outs, twists and turns and dips and doodles than the brain of Albert Einstein himself.

   _____

5. Others say his mouth was more grim than grin, that his eyes lit up like flashbulbs, because he knew he was finally facing a knot that would stand up and fight, a worthy *opponent.*

   _____

6. He would need the touch of a surgeon, the alertness of an owl, the *cunning* of three foxes and the foresight of a grand master in chess.

   _____

7. He would need the touch of a surgeon, the alertness of an owl, the cunning of three foxes and the *foresight* of a grand master in chess.

   _____

8. But nobody stepped off a curb, everybody kept moving north, an ugly, snarling black-and-white *escort* for the kid in the middle.

_____

Part II: Determining the Meaning   Match the vocabulary words to their dictionary definitions.

____ 1. dangled   A. skill in deception
____ 2. ranting   B. hung loosely
____ 3. incubating   C. looking into the future
____ 4. contortions   D. twisting and bending out of shape
____ 5. opponent   E. developing and hatching
____ 6. cunning   F. speaking in a violent manner
____ 7. foresight   G. one who is against another
____ 8. escort   H. a guide or guard

Maniac Magee Vocabulary Worksheets

Chapters 22-26
Part I: Using Prior Knowledge and Context Clues
Below are the sentences in which the vocabulary words appear in the text. Read the sentence. Use any clues you can find in the sentence combined with your prior knowledge, and write what you think the underlined words mean on the lines provided.

1. You have breakfast, *compliments* of mother's milk.

   _____

2. Maniac's answer was *prompt.*

   _____

3. *Dumbfounded,* the old man drove back out of the park to the nearest diner, where he sat with a cup of coffee while the boy wolfed down meatloaf and gravy, mashed potatoes, zucchini, salad, and coconut custard pie.

   _____

4. "The Blue Star treats every new *rookie* to his first meal in town free."

   _____

5. *Sleazy* hotels. *Sleazy* buses. *Sleazy* stadiums.

   _____

6. The *grizzled,* rickety coot showing the kid how to spray liners to the opposite field.

   _____

7. The grizzled, *rickety* coot showing the kid how to spray liners to the opposite field.

   _____

8. And every night, as the old man left for his room at the Y, he would *grouse*, "You ought to go to school."

_____

Part II: Determining the Meaning   Match the vocabulary words to their dictionary definitions.

_____ 1. compliments   A. acts of courtesy
_____ 2. prompt   B. streaked with gray
_____ 3. dumbfounded   C. astonished; amazed
_____ 4. rookie   D. complain; grumble
_____ 5. sleazy   E. instant; immediate
_____ 6. grizzled   F. shabby and dirty
_____ 7. rickety   G. shaky
_____ 8. grouse   H. a first year player

Maniac Magee Vocabulary Worksheets

Chapters 27-32
Part I: Using Prior Knowledge and Context Clues
Below are the sentences in which the vocabulary words appear in the text. Read the sentence. Use any clues you can find in the sentence combined with your prior knowledge, and write what you think the underlined words mean on the lines provided.

1. While he groused about so *preposterous* an idea, the kid laid down the mat he never used, bulldogged him down to it, pulled off his shoes, and draped a blanket over him.

   _____

2. The old man gave himself up willingly to his *exhaustion* and drifted off like a lazy, shy-high fly ball.

   _____

3. Maniac was jumping on his seat, screaming trash at Hands's *pursuers* every step to the goal line (and glancing about to make sure Mrs. Beale wasn't hearing.)

   _____

4. Maniac thought of Thanksgivings past, of sitting around a joyless table, his aunt and uncle as silent and lifeless as the *mammoth* bird they gnawed on.

   _____

5. By the time the two of them finished trimming it-- their tree-trimming instincts having *languished* for so many Christmases--hardly a pine needle could be seen under the tinsel and balls and whatnot.

   _____

6. They bundled themselves and *ventured* into the silent night.

   _____

7. Beyond the tall pines, stars glittered like snowflakes *reluctant* to fall.

   _____

8. He held the cold, limp hand that had thrown the pitch that had struck out Willie Mays, that had betrayed the old man's *stoic* ways by giving him a squeeze.

_____

Part II: Determining the Meaning Match the vocabulary words to their dictionary definitions.

____ 1. preposterous   A. complete weariness
____ 2. exhaustion   B. went in spite of risk
____ 3. pursuers   C. farfetched
____ 4. mammoth   D. indifferent to pleasure or pain
____ 5. languished   E. followers trying to overtake; chasers
____ 6. ventured   F. weakened; faded
____ 7. reluctant   G. unwilling
____ 8. stoic   H. gigantic; enormous

Maniac Magee Vocabulary Worksheets

Chapters 33-37
Part I: Using Prior Knowledge and Context Clues
Below are the sentences in which the vocabulary words appear in the text. Read the sentence. Use any clues you can find in the sentence combined with your prior knowledge, and write what you think the underlined words mean on the lines provided.

1. Maniac drifted from hour to hour, day to day, alone with his memories, a *stunned* and *solitary* wanderer.

   _____

2. Here the Continental Army had suffered through a winter of their own, and the vast, stark, frozen *desolation* itself seemed a more proper monument than statues and stones.

   _____

3. Maniac *confined* himself to three glasses of water and half a dozen Krimpets.

   _____

4. "Sure, John, you remember"--(wink, wink)--"at the Little League field the next day, you said I was lucky that all you threw me was fastballs, because you weren't ready to *reveal* your secret pitch, the one you'd been working on. Remember?"

   _____

5. Scene: McNab the father swaggers bare-armed out the front door, *bellowing* back, "Do yer homework!"

   _____

6. Russell and Piper lie *prone* at the hole.

   _____

7. He had suggested this feat himself, everyone else's _scoffing_--and, while the mother looked on, kissed the baby buffalo.

   _____

8. Other kids were always crowding around, _pelting_ him with questions.

   _____

9. And then one day they gave him the most _perilous_ challenge of all.

   _____

Part II: Determining the Meaning Match the vocabulary words to their dictionary definitions.

____ 1.	stunned	A.	yelling
____ 2.	desolation	B.	limited
____ 3.	confined	C.	jeering
____ 4.	reveal	D.	gloom; bleakness
____ 5.	bellowing	E.	dangerous
____ 6.	prone	F.	shocked
____ 7.	scoffing	G.	make known
____ 8.	perilous	H.	flat

Maniac Magee Vocabulary Worksheets

Chapters 38-41
Part I: Using Prior Knowledge and Context Clues
Below are the sentences in which the vocabulary words appear in the text. Read the sentence. Use any clues you can find in the sentence combined with your prior knowledge, and write what you think the underlined words mean on the lines provided.

1. They *halted* at the curb.

2. His only recollection was a feeling of sheer, joyful *exuberance*, himself in celebration: shouting "A-men!" in the Bethany Church.

3. Maniac kept moving, embarrassed, wishing he could just break out and sprint for the West End, wishing he could duck into the Beales' house and be sanctuaried there and not fear *reprisals* on them.

4. The reunion had been *ecstatic* and fearful and nonstop happy, and inside he was pure July.

5. Maniac couldn't help laughing. In spite of their twisted, *ludicrous* impressions of East Enders, the concern and the tears in their eyes had been genuine.

6. He could always *extort* a day or two in class from them with the free weekly pizza.

7. It was a maddening, *chaotic* time for Maniac.

8. Running in the mornings and reading in the afternoons gave him just enough *stability* to endure the zany nights at the McNabs'.

   _____

9. Running in the mornings and reading in the afternoons gave him just enough *stability* to *endure* the zany nights at the McNabs'.

   _____

10. In some *vague* way, to abandon the McNab boys would be to abandon something in himself.

    _____

Part II: Determining the Meaning   Match the vocabulary words to their dictionary definitions.

____ 1.	halted	A.	dependability
____ 2.	exuberance	B.	ridiculous
____ 3.	reprisals	C.	enthusiasm
____ 4.	ecstatic	D.	to bear with tolerance
____ 5.	ludicrous	E.	overjoyed
____ 6.	extort	F.	disorderly
____ 7.	chaotic	G.	unspecified
____ 8.	stability	H.	revenge
____ 9.	endure	I.	to get by threats
____ 10.	vague	J.	stopped

Maniac Magee Vocabulary Worksheets

Chapters 42-46
Part I: Using Prior Knowledge and Context Clues
Below are the sentences in which the vocabulary words appear in the text. Read the sentence. Use any clues you can find in the sentence combined with your prior knowledge, and write what you think the underlined words mean on the lines provided.

1. Maniac could feel the voltage that *surged* through Mars Bars and crackled black lightning from his eyes.

   _____

2. Mars Bar allowed himself to be dragged into them, but his jaw was *clenched* and his eyes kept straying to the gaping hole in the ceiling--and to the Cobras, who were slouching against the walls and baseboards, sipping beers and watching his every move.

   _____

3. The Cobras stayed, and Maniac, clamping the struggling Mars Bar for dear life, lugged him down a *gauntlet* of seething eyes to the door and the street.

   _____

4. The Cobras stayed, and Maniac, clamping the struggling Mars Bar for dear life, lugged him down a gauntlet of *seething* eyes to the door and the street.

   _____

5. Mars Bar *wrenched* free and stomped on ahead.

   _____

6. It may have been an *illusion*, but it seemed that the hungrier he got, the farther Mrs. Pickwell's whistle traveled.

   _____

7. This was the first in a series of apparently *random* mergings.

_____

8. Though each face showed no awareness of the other, they were in fact *minutely* sensitive to each other.

_____

Part II: Determining the Meaning Match the vocabulary words to their dictionary definitions.

____ 1. surged   A. without a specific pattern
____ 2. clenched   B. moved like waves
____ 3. gauntlet   C. violently excited
____ 4. seething   D. grasped tightly
____ 5. wrenched   E. fantasy; false belief
____ 6. illusion   F. an attack from all sides
____ 7. random   G. concerned with small details
____ 8. minutely   H. twisted

ANSWER KEY-PREREADING VOCABULARY WORKSHEETS *Maniac Magee*

Chapters 1-5
1. B
2. E
3. H
4. A
5. D
6. G
7. I
8. C
9. F
10. J

Chapters 6-11
1. D
2. I
3. C
4. G
5. J
6. B
7. F
8. H
9. A
10. E

Chapters 12-16
1. H
2. E
3. A
4. B
5. F
6. C
7. I
8. G
9. D

Chapters 17-21
1. B
2. F
3. E
4. D
5. G
6. A
7. C
8. H

Chapters 22-26
1. A
2. E
3. C
4. H
5. F
6. B
7. G
8. D

Chapters 27-32
1. C
2. A
3. E
4. H
5. F
6. B
7. G
8. D

Chapters 33-37
1. F
2. D
3. B
4. G
5. A
6. H
7. C
8. E

Chapters 38-41
1. J
2. C
3. H
4. E
5. B
6. I
7. F
8. A
9. D
10. G

Chapters 42-46
1. B
2. D
3. F
4. C
5. H
6. E
7. A
8. G

EXTRA VOCABULARY

The following words will not be tested. However, you may want to discuss their meanings with the students.

Chapters 1-5

1. There was a quick *smatter* of giggling by some people who figured the screaming kid was some part of the show, some funny animal maybe.

   slight knowledge

2. Yet there are other *theories*.

   explanations

3. A couple of people truly remember, and here's what they saw: a *scraggly* little kid jogging toward them.

   ragged; unkempt

4. Amanda was *suspicious*.

   distrustful

5. All *grungy*.

   dirty and rundown

6. It was the story of the *Children's Crusade.*

   During the Middle Ages, groups of Christians traveled from Europe to the Holy Land. The Children's Crusade occurred around 1212. Hundreds of children traveled from Germany to Italy, and planned to go on to Jerusalem to find Christ's burial vault. Most of the children either died during the journey to Italy or stayed in Italy.

7. It sailed back over the up-looking gym-classers, *spiraling* more perfectly than anything Brian Denehy had ever thrown, and landed in the outstretched hands of still stunned Hands Down.

   twisting and turning

8. Another swears it was a *mirage*, some sort of *hallucination*, possibly caused by evil *emanations* surrounding 803 Oriole Street.

   vision; fantasy
   apparition; illusion
   coming from a source

9. He's paralyzed, a mouse in front of the yawning *maw* of a python.

   throat

10. The phantom *Samaritan* stuck the book between his teeth, crouched down, hoisted Arnold Jones's limp *carcass* over his shoulder, and hauled him out of there like a sack of flour.

    A reference to a Bible story about a man from Samaria who stopped and helped another man.

    body

11. As the *stupefied* high-schoolers were leaving the scene, they looked back.

    astonished; shocked

Chapters 6-11

1. Just a punky, *runty* little kid, no Red Sox or Green Sox uniform.

   undersized; small

2. He couldn't stand having this *blemish* on his record.

   defect; imperfection

3. Then suddenly he stopped *glaring*, suddenly he was smiling.

   staring in an unpleasant way

4. The chin *jutted* out more. "Tell me I'm bad."

   stuck out

Chapters 12-16
1. So quiet you could hear the water running far below the sewer grates while the sun *shinnied* up the rain spouts.

   climbed up

Chapters 17-21
1. He did accept an orange soda, though, and then a little kid, whose sneaker laces Maniac had untied many a time, handed up to him a three-pack of *Tastykake Butterscotch Krimpets*.

   Tastykake is a brand name for small snack cakes and cookies. The company originated in Philadelphia and distributes mostly in that area and in some other Middle Atlantic States. Butterscotch Krimpets are a small, rectangular vanilla sponge cakes with butterscotch frosting, sold in packs of three.

Chapters 22-26
1. The grizzled, rickety *coot* showing the kid how to spray liners to the opposite field.

   a foolish, eccentric, old person

2. Maniac knew that most if not all of that was *blarney,* and just to make sure, he watched the ball extra carefully.

   deceptive nonsense

Chapters 27-32
1. Maniac went to the bookcase that served as a *pantry*.

   a room or closet used to store food

2. Maniac thought of Thanksgivings past, of sitting around a joyless table, his aunt and uncle as silent and lifeless as the mammoth bird they *gnawed* on.

   bit; chewed

3. Of course, one cannot listen to *polka* music for long before getting up and dancing, which is what the two thanksgivers did as soon as their *bloated* stomach allowed.

   a lively round dance done by couples

   swollen

4. Thanks to his long *acquaintanceship* with the locker room attendant, he and Maniac were privileged to continue using the Y's shower facilities at their pleasure.

   knowing someone

5. In the pine-patched moonlight, the Queen Anne's goblets looked for all the world like *filigreed* silver.

   delicate ornamental work made from gold, silver, or other fine twisted wire

6. The *pallbearers* were unknown to Maniac.

   persons carrying a coffin at a funeral

7. Maniac was the only *mourner*.

   a person showing grief at a funeral

Chapters 33-37
1. Maniac drifted from hour to hour, day to day, alone with his memories, a *stunned* and solitary wanderer.

   overwhelmed or dazed

2. Here the Continental Army had suffered through a winter of their own, and the *vast, stark*, frozen desolation itself seemed a more proper monument than statues and stones.

   very large in area

   harsh, grim

3. Scene: McNab the father *swaggers* bare-armed out the front door, bellowing back, "Do yer homework!"

   to walk with a strut

4. Dreams pursued memories, courted and danced and coupled with them and they became one, and the *gaunt, beseeching phantoms* that called to him had the rag-wrapped feet of Washington's *regulars* and the faces of his mother and father and Aunt Dot and Uncle Dan and the Beales and Earl Grayson

   a soldier who belongs to a regular army

5. In that bedeviled army there would be no more *recruits*.

   people who are enrolled for military service

6. Soon the three of them were trekking past the Washington Memorial Chapel, Russell and Piper with their bag, Maniac with his *satchel*.

   a small bag with a shoulder strap, used for carrying books or clothing

7. "What was the pitch? What was the pitch?" chanted the *urchins.*

   mischievous or playful children

8. They tore into the bag like jackals into *carrion*.

   dead or decaying flesh

9. Other kids were always crowding around, *pelting* them with questions.

   hitting repeatedly

10. The only sounds were inside their heads--the moaning and wailing of the ghosts of all the poor slobs who had ever *blundered* onto Finsterwald's property.

moved clumsily

Chapters 38-41
1. He gave a sniff; his smile went a little *smirky*.

an offensively self-satisfied smile

2. These were heavy considerations, heavy enough to slow him down--until the hysterical crowd and the sight of Mars Bar's sneaker bottoms and the boiling of his own blood *ignited* his afterburners, and before you could say, "Burn 'im, Magee."

set fire to; caused to burn

3. Maniac kept moving, embarrassed, wishing he could just break out and sprint for the West End, wishing he could duck into the Beales' house and be *sanctuaried* there and not fear reprisals on them.

given a safe place to stay

5. He took them to the library, then scrapped that idea after their *shenanigans* left the librarian blubbering and blue-faced.

mischievous tricks or pranks

Chapters 42-46
1. Maniac could feel the voltage that *surged* through Mars Bars and crackled black lightning from his eyes.

suddenly increased

2. This was the first in a series of apparently random *mergings*.

combining

3. They jogged silently for a block, then *veered* apart.

turned aside

The next time they *dovetailed*, they stayed that way for two blocks, then three blocks, and so on.

combined into a whole

DAILY LESSONS

LESSON ONE

Student Objectives
  1. To preview the *Maniac Magee* Unit
  2. To receive books and other related materials (study guides, reading assignment)
  3. To relate prior knowledge to the new material
  4. To discuss one of the major themes of the novel (prejudice) by participating in a group activity
  5. To discuss the characteristics of mythology and compare them to reality

Activity #1

Make an even number of small squares of either green and purple construction paper. Give green squares to half of the class and purple to the other. Tell all of the students with green papers to sit on one side of the room, and the students with the purple papers to sit on the other side. Put a barrier, such as a piece of masking tape, down the center of the room. Then tell the students they are not allowed to cross the barrier. Tell the students in the purple group that the students in the green group are strange: they don't brush their teeth, they eat with their hands; they beat up students with purple papers. Then tell the students in the green group the same things about the purple group. Ask students what they know about each other, how they found it out, and whether or not they would want to cross the barrier. Then ask students what this exercise reminded them of. If no one suggests prejudice, explain it yourself. Tell students one of the themes in Maniac Magee is prejudice between the black and the white people in the town.

Activity #2

Distribute the materials students will use in this unit. Explain in detail how students are to use these materials.

Study Guides Students should preview the study guide questions before each reading assignment to get a feeling for what events and ideas are important in that section. After reading the section, students will (as a class or individually) answer the questions to review the important events and ideas from that section of the book. Students should keep the study guides as study materials for the unit test.

Reading Assignment Sheet You need to fill in the reading assignment sheet to let students know when their reading has to be completed. You can either write the assignment sheet on a side blackboard or bulletin board and leave it there for students to see each day, or you can duplicate copies for each student to have. In either case, you should advise students to become very familiar with the reading assignments so they know what is expected of them.

Unit Outline You may find it helpful to distribute copies of the Unit Outline to your students so they can keep track of upcoming lessons and assignments. You may also want to post a copy of the Unit Outline on a bulletin board and cross off each lesson as you complete it.

Extra Activities Center The Unit Resources portion of this unit contains suggestions for a library of related books and articles in your classroom as well as crossword and word search puzzles. Make an extra activities center in your room where you will keep these materials for students to use. Bring the books and articles in from the library and keep several copies of the puzzles on hand. Explain to students that these materials are available for students to use when they finish reading assignments or other class work early.

Books Each school has its own rules and regulations regarding student use of school books. Advise students of the procedures that are normal for your school.

Notebook or Unit Folder You may want the students to keep all of their worksheets, notes, and other papers for the unit together in a binder or notebook. During the first class meeting, tell them how you want them to arrange the folder. Make divider pages for vocabulary worksheets, prereading study guide questions, review activities, notes, and tests. You may want to give a grade for accuracy in keeping the folder.

Activity #3

Do a group KWL Sheet with the students (form included.) Some students will know something about Jerry Spinelli or his books and will have information to share. Put this information in the K column (What I Know.) Ask students what they want to find out from reading the book and record this in the W column (What I Want to Find Out.) Keep the sheet and refer back to it after reading the book. Complete the L column (What I Learned) at that time.

Activity #4

Read the first two pages of the story, "Before the Story," aloud to students. Tell them a myth is a traditional, typically ancient story dealing with supernatural beings, ancestors, or heroes that serves as an explanation of aspects of the natural world or the customs or ideals of society. It can be a story, a theme, an object, or a character that symbolizes some aspect of a culture. Myths are often based on a true story or event, with some elements made up or exaggerated. Invite students to discuss myths with which they are familiar.

Discuss the meaning of Spinelli's message in "Before the Story". Tell students to look for the elements that they think are myth, and the ones they think are more realistic. Also tell them they will discuss this in depth at the end of the story.

KWL *Maniac Magee*

Directions: Before reading, think about what you already know about Jerry Spinelli and/or *Maniac Magee*. Write the information in the K column. Think about what you would like to find out from reading the book. Write your questions in the W column. After you have read the book, use the L column to write the answers to your questions from the W column, and anything else you remember from the book.

K **What I Know**	**W** **What I Want to Find Out**	**L** **What I Learned**

LESSON TWO

Student Objectives:
1. To become familiar with the vocabulary for Chapters 1-5
2. To preview the study questions for Chapters 1-5
3. To read Chapters 1-5
4. To review the main ideas and themes in Chapters 1-5

Activity #1

Work through the prereading vocabulary worksheet for Chapters 1-5 with the students. Tell them they will have a sheet like this to complete before reading each section of the book.

Activity #2

Show students how to preview the study questions for Chapters 1-5 of *Manic Magee*. Encourage students to predict what they think answers might be, to write down their predictions, and to compare these with their answers after reading the chapters.

Activity #3

Read Chapter 1 aloud to the students. Then invite individuals to continue reading Chapters 2-5 aloud to the class as they follow along in their books.

Activity #4

Work through the answers to the study guide questions with the class. Discuss the answers in detail. Write the answers on the board or overhead projector transparencies so students can have the correct answers for study purposes. Encourage students to take notes. If students own their copies of *Maniac Magee*, suggest that they use high lighter pens in different colors to mark important passages and vocabulary words, and to answer study guide questions.

Note: It is a good practice in public speaking and leadership skills for individual students to take charge of leading the discussion of the study questions. Perhaps a different student could go to the front of the class and lead the discussion each day that the study questions are discussed during this unit. Of course, the teacher should guide the discussion when appropriate and be sure to fill in any gaps the students leave.

LESSON THREE

Student Objectives
    1. To become familiar with the vocabulary for Chapters 6-11
    2. To preview the study questions for Chapters 6-11
    3. To read Chapters 6-11 aloud for evaluation
    4. To discuss the foreshadowing in Chapter 8

Activity #1

    Have students work with a partner and go over the vocabulary and study guide questions for Chapters 6-11.

Activity #2

    Tell students their oral reading ability will be evaluated. Show them copies of the Oral Reading Evaluation Form and discuss it. Model correct intonation and expression by reading the first few paragraphs of Chapter 6 aloud. Call on individual students to read a few paragraphs aloud. Encourage the other students to follow along in their books. If you have a student who is unwilling or unable to read in front of the class, make arrangements to do his or her evaluation privately at another time.

Activity #3

    Have students stop reading after they finish Chapter 8. Call attention to the foreshadowing at the end of the chapter. Have students predict what the unexpected turn might be.

ORAL READING EVALUATION *Maniac Magee*

Name_____ Class_____ Date_____

SKILL	EXCELLENT	GOOD	AVERAGE	FAIR	POOR
FLUENCY	5	4	3	2	1
CLARITY	5	4	3	2	1
AUDIBILITY	5	4	3	2	1
PRONUNCIATION	5	4	3	2	1
_____	5	4	3	2	1
_____	5	4	3	2	1

TOTAL _____ GRADE _____

COMMENTS:

LESSON FOUR

Student Objectives
1. To review the main ideas and themes in Chapters 6-11
2. To practice writing to persuade

Activity #1

Invite students to work in small groups to either dramatize or illustrate the answer to one of the study guide questions. Allow time for each group to present their answer.

Activity #2

Write the word persuade on the chalkboard and ask students what it means. Dramatize by pretending a student has a ticket to a concert you want to go to, and asking that student to give you the ticket. Have them find examples in Chapters 1-11 of *Maniac Magee* when Jeffrey tried to persuade someone to do something. (In Chapter 1, he yelled "Talk! Talk, will ya! Talk! Talk! Talk!") to his aunt and uncle. In Chapter 3 he persuaded Amanda to loan him a book.) Brainstorm a list of times when the students might want to persuade someone to do something their way, or persuade someone to give them something. Tell them they will write a persuasive letter or short speech.

Activity #3

Distribute copies of Writing Assignment #1. Go over the assignment in detail with the students. Tell them they will have the remainder of the class period to begin working on the assignment. Give the due date for the completed assignment. It should be a few days before the writing conferences, which are scheduled for Lesson 9.

Activity #4

Distribute copies of the Writing Evaluation Form (included with this Unit Plan.) Explain to students that during Lesson 9 you will be holding individual writing conferences about the assignment. Make sure students are familiar with the criteria on the Writing Evaluation Form.

Activity #5

You may want to leave time during one class period for students to read their persuasive letters or act out their speeches.

Follow Up: After you have graded the assignments, have a writing conference with each student. This Unit Plan schedules one in Lesson 9. After the writing conference, allow students to revise their papers using your suggestions to complete the revisions. Grade the revisions on an A-C-E scale: A = all revisions well done; C = some revisions made; E = few or no revisions made. This will speed your grading time and still give some credit for the students' efforts.

WRITING ASSIGNMENT #1 *Maniac Magee*
Writing to Persuade

PROMPT
Jeffrey wanted to borrow one of Amanda's books. Amanda never lent her books to anyone, but he persuaded her to lend him one. Your assignment is to persuade someone to do something you want. You can either write a letter or prepare a speech to present in person.

PREWRITING
Choose one of the topics from the brainstorm list, or think of another one on your own. Make a list of the reasons someone should do what you want. Then number the reasons in order from most to least important. Under each reason, think of supporting statements to go along with it.

DRAFTING
Make an introductory statement in which you state your request. Use one paragraph for each of your reasons. Use the supporting statements for each reason. Summarize your request in the closing paragraph.

PEER EDITING /REVISING
When you finish the first draft, ask another student to look at it. You may want to give the student your notes so he/she can double check for you and see that you have included all of the information. After reading, he or she should tell you what he/she liked best about your persuasive speech or letter, which parts were difficult to understand or need more information, and ways in which your work could be improved. Reread your persuasive speech or letter considering your critic's comments and make the corrections you think are necessary.

PROOFREADING
Do a final proofreading of your persuasive speech/letter. Double check your grammar, spelling, organization, and the clarity of your ideas.

FINAL DRAFT
Follow your teacher's guidelines for completing the final draft of your paper.

WRITING EVALUATION FORM *Maniac Magee*

Name _____ Date _____ Class _____

Writing Assignment # _____

Circle One For Each Item:

Composition	excellent	good	fair	poor
Style	excellent	good	fair	poor
Grammar	excellent	good	fair	poor (errors noted)
Spelling	excellent	good	fair	poor (errors noted)
Punctuation	excellent	good	fair	poor (errors noted)
Legibility	excellent	good	fair	poor (errors noted)

Strengths:

Weaknesses:

Comments/Suggestions:

LESSON FIVE

Student Objectives
    1. To analyze examples of cause and effect in the story
    2. To become familiar with the vocabulary for Chapters 12-16
    3. To preview the study questions for Chapters 12-16
    4. To silently read Chapters 12-16
    5. To discuss the foreshadowing at the end of Chapter 16 and make a prediction
    6. To review the main themes and ideas in Chapters 12-16

Activity #1 Minilesson: Cause and Effect
    Introduce the concept of cause and effect by using examples with which they are familiar, such as the following: 1) a snowstorm leaves 10 inches of snow in the area (cause), so the schools are closed (effect); 2) a student pays attention in class, studies, and does all assignments (cause), so the student passes a big test (effect); 3) a person forgets to water the plants (cause) and they all die(effect.)
    Tell students they will be looking at examples of cause and effect in the chapters they have read so far in *Maniac Magee*. Ask them to look at Chapter 1. Remind students that Jeffrey ran away from the concert, and from his aunt and uncle. Tell them that was the effect, and ask them to find the cause. (Students will have to infer the main cause, that Jeffrey didn't want to continue living under the conditions at his aunt and uncle's house.)
    Have students continue to find examples of cause/effect in Chapters 1-11. You may want to list them on a chart or on the chalkboard. Tell students to look for more examples after they read Chapters 12-16.

Activity #2
    Give students about fifteen minutes to complete the prereading vocabulary worksheet and study guide questions. You may want to let them work with a partner or in a small group for this activity.

Activity #3
    Ask students to silently read Chapters 12-16, and answer the study questions as they read.

Activity #4
    Call attention to the last two paragraphs in Chapter 16. Ask students to predict how Maniac will be able to see the dislike.

Activity #5
    Have students trade study guide papers with a partner and check each other's answers.

Activity #6
    Have students predict how Maniac finally is able to see the dislike around him.
Note: Tell students they will be having a quiz during Lesson 7, when they have finished reading Part 1, Chapters 1-21.

LESSON SIX

Student Objectives
1. To become familiar with the vocabulary for Chapters 17-21
2. To preview the study questions for Chapters 17-21
3. To silently read Chapters 17-21
4. To review the main themes and ideas in Chapters 17-21
5. To identify and discuss the descriptions, similes and metaphors in the story so far

Activity #1
Divide the students into pairs or small groups. Give each group one vocabulary word to define. Then have each group teach their word to the rest of the class.

Activity #2
Read over the study guide questions with the students and ask them to predict the answers.

Activity #3
Have students read the chapters silently. If there are a few students who have difficulty, take them aside and read with them.

Activity #4
Discuss the answers to the study guide questions with the students.

Activity #5
Call attention to the descriptions of the heat on the first page of Chapter 17. Tell the students these are examples of exaggeration. Ask them to make up a few examples of their own.

Activity #6 Minilesson: Simile and Metaphor
Read the simile on the first page of Chapter 17 aloud "the fire hydrant at Green and Chestnut was gushing like Niagara Falls." Tell them it is a simile. A simile is a comparison using the words *like* or *as*. Ask students to explain the meaning, or draw a picture to illustrate it. Then read the descriptions of Cobble's Knot in Chapter 20, "It was a frizzy globe", "a gigantic hairball." Tell students these descriptions are metaphors. A metaphor compares one thing to another without using the words *like* or *as*. You may want to use the Simile/Metaphor chart to have the students keep track of the similes and metaphors they find in the novel.

Note: Remind students they will have a quiz on Part 1, Chapters 1-21, during the next class meeting. Suggest that they review all of their notes and study guide questions and answers.

SIMILE / METAPHOR CHART

Directions: Find examples of similes and metaphors in *Maniac Magee*. Write down the chapter and page number. Copy the phrase, and them write the meaning. Then put a check mark in either the simile (S) or metaphor (M) column.

Ch./Pg.	Phrase	Meaning	S	M

Draw or cut out a picture to illustrate one of the similes or metaphors from the novel.

LESSON SEVEN

Student Objectives
    1. To take a quiz on Part 1, Chapters 1-21
    2. To become familiar with the vocabulary for Chapters 22-26
    3. To preview the study questions for Chapters 22-26
    4. To read Chapters 22-26 with a partner

Activity #1 Quiz

    Distribute quizzes (multiple choice study questions from Chapters 1-21) and give students about fifteen minutes to complete them. Collect the papers for grading.

Activity #2

    Before having students complete the prereading vocabulary worksheet, list the words on the board. Invite students to tell what they think the words mean. Then have the students complete the worksheet. They can compare their guesses to the actual meanings of the words.

Activity #3

    Have students discuss the prereading study questions with a partner, and record their predictions.

Activity #4

    Invite students to either read the chapters silently or read them aloud quietly with a partner. If they finish reading early, they can work on the answers to the study questions. Tell them to have the answers completed before the next class meeting.

LESSON EIGHT

Student Objectives
    1. To review the main ideas and events in Chapters 22-26
    2. To become familiar with the vocabulary for Chapters 27-32
    3. To preview the study questions for Chapters 27-32
    4. To read Chapters 27-32 silently
    5. To analyze the character traits of Jeffrey and Grayson

Activity #1

    Go over the answers to the study guide questions. Have students prove their answers by reading the appropriate paragraphs from the text aloud.

Activity #2

    Give students about fifteen minutes to complete the prereading vocabulary worksheet and preview the study guide questions for Chapters 27-32.

Activity #3 Minilesson: Character Traits

    Explain that an author creates characters, in this case Jeffrey Magee and Grayson, by giving them traits such as physical attributes, thoughts, and feelings. The author develops these traits by telling what the characters say, do, and think. Writers usually base their characters at least in part on a real person or persons, and then elaborate.

    Distribute copies of the Character Traits Chart. Work with the students to discuss some of Jeffrey's character traits, and record the information. Tell students they should continue to be aware of Jeffrey's character as they read the next section, and add to the character map.

    Distribute copies of the Character Traits Chart. Tell students to complete it for Grayson and bring it to the next class.

Activity #4

    Give the students the rest of the period to read silently and work on the Character Traits Charts.

LESSON NINE

Student Objectives
1. To participate in a writing conference with the teacher
2. To revise Writing Assignment #1 based on the conference
3. To become familiar with the vocabulary for Chapters 33-37
4. To preview the study questions for Chapters 33-37
5. To read Chapters 33-37 silently

Activity #1
    Find a quiet corner of the classroom and hold individual writing conferences. Tell the students to work independently on the other assignments.

Activity #2
    Distribute copies of the prereading vocabulary worksheet and study guide questions for Chapters 33-37. Tell students to complete them and then read Chapters 33-37 silently.

Activity #3
    Allow time for students to work on revising Writing Assignment #1, or give this as a homework assignment.

CHARACTER TRAITS CHART
Maniac Magee

CHARACTER _____

Trait _____	Trait _____	Trait _____	Trait _____
Events That Show It	Events That Show It	Events That Show It	Events That Show It

LESSON TEN

Student Objectives
    1. To review the main ideas and themes in Chapters 33-37
    2. To become familiar with the non-fiction writing assignment

Activity #1

    Give each student four 1" x 2" strips of colored paper or index cards--one blue, one yellow, one green, one pink. Have them put a large letter A on the blue paper, B on the yellow, C on the green, and D on the pink. Distribute copies of the Multiple Choice/Quiz questions for Chapters 33-37. Ask students to read the first question and hold up the colored paper for the correct answer. Then have them mark the correct answers on their worksheet.

Activity #2

    Distribute copies of the Nonfiction Assignment sheet and go over it in detail with the students. Explain to students that they each are to read at least one nonfiction piece, write a report about it, and fill in the Nonfiction Assignment Sheet. The report will count as one of the three unit writing assignments, Writing to Inform. They will also present their information to the class in the form of an oral report during Lesson 18. The nonfiction piece could be a book, a magazine article, or information from an encyclopedia or the Internet. Also consider letting students watch an educational television show or video, such as a documentary. Give them the due date for the assignment.

    Encourage students to read about topics that are related to the themes of the novel. Some suggestions are: racial prejudice, the problems facing orphaned children, homelessness, segregation, and illiteracy.

Activity #3

    Distribute copies of Writing Assignment #2. Go over the assignment in detail with the students. Tell them they will have the remainder of the class period to begin working on the assignment.

NONFICTION ASSIGNMENT SHEET *Maniac Magee*
(To be completed after reading the required nonfiction article)

Name _____ Date _____ Class _____

Title of Nonfiction Read _____

Written By _____ Publication Date _____

I. Factual Summary: Write a short summary of the piece you read.

II. Vocabulary:
    1. Which vocabulary words were difficult?

    2. What did you do to help yourself understand the words?

III. Interpretation: What was the main point the author wanted you to get from reading his/her work?

IV. Criticism:
    1. Which points of the piece did you agree with or find easy to believe? Why?

    2. With which points of the piece did you disagree or find difficult to believe? Why?

V. Personal Response:
    1. What do you think about this piece?

    2. How does this piece help you better understand the novel *Maniac Magee*?

WRITING ASSIGNMENT #2 *Maniac Magee*
Writing to Inform

PROMPT

You are reading about Jeffrey Lionel Magee, a young boy who was orphaned at the age of 3. You read about the problems he had living with his aunt and uncle, as well as his living conditions after he left them. You also read about the way the black and white neighborhoods were segregated, or separated from each other. Your assignment is to find out more about one of these topics, or about another one in the book that interests you.

PREWRITING

Choose a topic or topics that interest you. Go to the library and find as many sources as you can on the topic. Look for encyclopedias, books, magazine articles, videos, and Internet sources. You may want to interview an expert on the topic of your choice.

Think of questions you have about your topic. Write each one on a separate index card. Then read to find the answers, and write them on the cards. Also take notes on interesting and important facts, even if you did not have questions about them. Put each fact on a separate card. Make sure to cite your references. That means to write down the source and the page number for each one. Arrange your note card in the order you want to use for your paper, and number them.

DRAFTING

Introduce your topic in the first paragraph. Tell why you chose it, and give a preview of what the rest of the paper will be about. Then write several paragraphs about the topic. Each paragraph should have a main idea and supporting details. Your last paragraph should summarize the information in the report.

PEER CONFERENCE/REVISING

When you finish the rough draft, ask another student to look at it. You may want to give the student your note cards so he/she can double check for you and see that you have included all of the information. After reading, he or she should tell you what he/she liked best about your report, which parts were difficult to understand or needed more information, and ways in which your work could be improved. Reread your report considering your critic's comments and make the corrections you think are necessary.

PROOFREADING/EDITING

Do a final proofreading of your report, double-checking your grammar, spelling, organization, and the clarity of your ideas.

FINAL DRAFT

Follow your teacher's directions for making a final copy of your report.

LESSON ELEVEN

<u>Student Objectives</u>
1. To become familiar with the vocabulary for Chapters 38-41
2. To preview the study questions for Chapters 38-41
3. To read Chapters 38-41
4. To make predictions about events in the chapters
5. To practice reading dialog aloud
6. To retell the main events to a small group of students

<u>Activity #1</u>

Give students about 15 minutes to complete the prereading vocabulary worksheet and look over the study questions.

<u>Activity #2</u>

Since these chapters contain a lot of dialog, you may wish to assign parts and have students take turns reading aloud. Encourage them to read with expression.

<u>Activity # 3</u>

Have the students stop reading at the end of Chapter 40. Ask students to predict whom Maniac will bring to the party, and why.

<u>Activity #4</u>

After the students have read the chapters, have them form small groups. Tell one student to begin retelling the events in the chapters, starting with Chapter 38. Have that student tell as much as he/she remembers, then have another student continue from where the first left off. Invite students to add information to the retelling. Encourage them to also discuss their personal reactions to the events tin these chapters.

<u>Activity #5</u>

Assign the study guide questions to be completed before the next class meeting.

LESSON TWELVE

Student Objectives
1. To review the main ideas and themes in Chapters 38-41
2. To become familiar with the vocabulary for Chapters 42-46
3. To preview the study questions for Chapters 42-46
4. To make predictions about the outcome of the book
5. To read Chapters 42-46

Activity #1
Go over the answers to the study guide questions.

Activity #2
Give students about 15 minutes to complete the prereading vocabulary worksheet and look over the study guide questions.

Activity #3
Ask students to predict what will happen in these chapters. Discuss what might happen to Jeffrey: where he will live, if he will stay in Two Mills or move on. Tell them to base their answers on clues from the vocabulary words and the study questions.

Activity #4
Have the students read Chapters 42-46 silently, or ask students to read aloud, depending on the needs of your group. Tell students to answer the study questions in time for the next class meeting.

LESSON THIRTEEN

Student Objectives
    1. To review the main ideas and themes in Chapters 42-46.
    2. To complete a story map

Activity #1
    Ask students to work in small groups and discuss the answers to the study questions. Circulate among the groups and add information to their answers as necessary.

Activity #2
    Distribute copies of the Story Map. Tell students the story map includes all of the elements of a fictional story: characters, setting, problem or conflict, events, and solution or resolution. Help students fill in the details on the story map. Encourage them to reread the text to find details for the map.

Alternate Activity
    Instead of using the Story Map to cover the entire story, assign small groups of students to complete a map for each of the reading assignment sections. Then have each group present their information in order according to the story chapters. This will serve as a good review of the main ideas and events in the novel.

LESSON FOURTEEN

Student Objectives
    1. To construct Clerihew and acrostic poems
    2. To share the poems with other students

Activity #1
    Distribute copies of Writing Assignment #3. Go over the instructions in detail. You may want to model writing one of each of the poems first. Give students the remainder of the period to work on their poems. If more time is necessary, set a due date for the assignment.

Activity #2
    Invite students to have a poetry reading and share their poems with each other.

STORY MAP
Maniac Magee

```
┌─────────────────────────────┐      ┌─────────────────────────────┐
│        CHARACTERS           │      │          SETTING            │
│ Main                        │      │ Time                        │
│                             │      │                             │
│                             │      │                             │
│ Minor                       │      │ Place                       │
│                             │      │                             │
└─────────────────────────────┘      └─────────────────────────────┘

┌─────────────────────────────┐      ┌─────────────────────────────┐
│          THEME              │      │       POINT OF VIEW         │
│                             │      │                             │
│                             │      │                             │
└─────────────────────────────┘      └─────────────────────────────┘

┌─────────────────────────────┐
│         PROBLEM             │
│                             │
│                             │
└─────────────────────────────┘

            ┌─────────────────────────────────────┐
            │              EVENTS                 │
            │                                     │
            │                                     │
            │                                     │
            │                                     │
            │                                     │
            └─────────────────────────────────────┘

                          ┌─────────────────────────────┐
                          │          SOLUTION           │
                          │                             │
                          └─────────────────────────────┘
```

WRITING ASSIGNMENT #3 *Maniac Magee*
Writing to Express a Personal Opinion

PROMPT

Now that you have finished reading Maniac Magee, you have probably formed an opinion about the characters and events. This is your opportunity to express your opinions. You will write two poems about characters or events in the novel.

One poem will be a Clerihew. The Clerihew was invented by E. Clerihew Bentley. It is a poem about a person., and can be serious or funny. It has 4 lines, with 2 rhyming couplets. Lines 1 and 2 rhyme, and lines 3 and 4 rhyme. The first line is a person's name. The name can be listed either last name first (Magee, Jeffrey) or first name and then last (Jeffrey Magee). A sample Clerihew is at the bottom of the page.

The other poem will be an acrostic. An acrostic poem describes a noun. Write the noun vertically (up and down) on the left side of the paper. You may want to make it larger than the rest of the print, or decorate the letters. Brainstorm words about the noun that begin with the letters in the word. Choose the words that combine to make the best description. You can make short, one or two word descriptions, or write full sentences. A sample acrostic is at the bottom of thepage.

PREWRITING

Make a list of possible topics for your poems. You may want to look over your study guide questions to find topics. After you make your list, choose the two you want to write about.

DRAFTING

Make a first draft of one poem. Experiment with different words. Then make a draft of the second poem.

PEER CONFERENCING/ REVISING

When you finish the rough drafts, ask another student to look at them. You may want to read your poems aloud to the student. After reading or listening, the student should tell you what he/she liked best about your poems, which parts were hard to understand or need more information, and ways in which your work could be improved. Reread your poems considering your critic's comments and make any changes you think are necessary.

PROOFREADING/EDITING

Do a final proofreading of your poems, double checking your grammar, spelling, organization, and a the clarity of your ideas.

FINAL DRAFT

Follow your teacher's guidelines for completing the final draft of your poems.

Sample Clerihew	Sample Acrostic
Jeffrey Lionel Magee Had athletic ability. He'd kick, jump, and run But not always for fun.	**M**et a lot of people in Two Mills. **A**unt Dot shared him with Uncle Dan. **N**ever gave up his dreams. **I**nfluenced people on both sides of Hector Street. **A**manda was his friend. **C**ared about his friends.

LESSON FIFTEEN

Student Objective
To discuss *Maniac Magee* at the interpretive and critical levels

Activity #1
Choose the questions from the Extra Writing Assignment/Discussion Questions which seem most appropriate for your students. A class discussion of these questions is most effective if students have been given the opportunity to formulate answers to the questions prior to the discussion. To this end, you may either have all the students answer all the questions, divide the class into groups and assign one or more questions to each group, or you could assign one question to each student in your class. The option you choose will make a difference in the amount of class time needed for this activity.

Activity #2
After students have had ample time to answer the questions, begin your class discussion. Be sure students take notes during the discussion so they have information to study for the unit test.

EXTRA WRITING ASSIGNMENT/DISCUSSION QUESTIONS

Interpretation

1. From what point of view is the story written? How does this affect our understanding of the story?

2. What are the main conflicts in the story? Are they resolved? If so, how? If not, why not?

3. What is the setting of the story? How important is the setting to the story?

4. Write a character sketch of one of the following: Jeffrey Magee, Amanda Beale, Mars Bar Thompson, John McNab, Grayson.

5. How old was Jeffrey when he ran away from Hollidaysburg? Chapter 1

6. How do you think Jeffrey felt while he was living with his aunt and uncle? Chapter 1

7. What do you think Aunt Dot and Uncle Dan did after Jeffrey ran away?

8. What do you think Jeffrey did for the year it took him to get from Hollidaysburg to Two Mills?

9. Why do you think Jeffrey stayed in Two Mills? Chapter 2

10. Why do you think Amanda lent a book to Jeffrey? Chapter 3

11. Why was Amanda so surprised to see Jeffrey? Chapter 3

12. What does the phrase "cool times ten" in Chapter 5 mean? Write other phrases that could have the same meaning?

13. Why was Jeffrey so fascinated by the story of the Children's Crusade? Chapter 8

14. What do you think Maniac felt like doing to the lady who put the broom between him and Mars Bar? Why? Chapter 10

15. How do you think Maniac felt while he was living with the Beales? Chapter 13-15

16. How do you think Maniac learned to behave in a family when he didn't have one? Ch. 13

17. In Chapter 16, Spinelli says ,"Maniac Magee was blind. Sort of." What does he mean? Why didn't Maniac see the clues that Spinelli shows the readers?

18. How did the Beale family members feel when they saw the writing on the side of their house? Chapter 18

19. How did Maniac feel when he saw the writing on the side of the house? Chapter 18

20. Why do you think Jeffrey went back to the Beales' house after he had gone? Chapter 18

21. What did the scene at the end of Chapter 21, when Maniac was leaving town, say about the people involved?

22. What was the "worm of an idea" that Grayson had? Chapter 23

23. How did learning to read change Grayson's life? Chapter 28

24. How old is Grayson? Chapter 28

25. Why did Maniac sleep in a different backyard every night? Chapter 44

26. Why did Mars Bar rescue Russell? Chapter 45

27. What was the hardest thing for Jeffrey to deal with? Why do you think so?

Critical
1. Is the story believable? Why or why not?

2. The introduction says that it's hard to know what's true and what's a myth. Which parts do you think could be true? Which could be a myth?

3. From what point of view is the story written? Is this effective? Would another point of view work as well?

4. How did Jeffrey change over the course of the novel?

5. Which other characters showed changes? What were the changes?

6. What was the overall mood of the story? Give examples to support your answer.

7. What point is Jerry Spinelli trying to make with Maniac's first conversation with Mars Bar on Chapter 10? Is it effective?

8. What is Jerry Spinelli saying about prejudice? Is it effective?

9. Reread Chapter 10, when Maniac meets Mars Bar for the first time. Spinelli uses two meanings of the word "bad." Is this effective? Why did Spinelli include this scene?

Critical
10. Which of Maniac's relationships (with Grayson, Amanda, Mars Bar, the McNab boys) was most fully developed? Use examples to support your answer.

11. Examine Spinelli's use of descriptive language. Discuss some effective examples.

12. Which of Maniac's relationships changed the most during the novel?

13. Trace the changes in the racial relationships in the novel.

14. Spinelli gives the location of the story, but not the year. Why did he omit this? Does not knowing the year affect your understanding or enjoyment of the story? In what year do you think the story took place? Why?

15. Jerry Spinelli often uses vivid language to describe a scene or an event. Give an example of his use of vivid language that you thought was effective. Tell why it was effective.

16. Could any of the main events be left out? If so, which ones? If not, why not?

17. What problem or conflict does Spinelli use to get the story started? How effective is it?

18. Could you change the order of the main events and still have the same outcome? If not, how would the outcome change if the order of events were changed?

19. How would the story have to change to have a different ending?

20. How would the story change if there were a different narrator?

21. Which character do you know the most about? Which do you know the least about?

22. Discuss Spinelli's use of language. Is it natural? Do people you know talk the way the characters did?

23. Does the mood of the story change? How does the author show this?

24. Which chapter was the most important? Why?

Personal Response
1. Did you enjoy reading *Maniac Magee*? Why or why not?

2. Is *Maniac Magee* an effective title for the book? Why or why not? If not, what title would you suggest?

3. What do you think Jeffrey will do next? Why?

4. Did Jeffrey's experiences change the way you look at yourself or your life? Explain.

5. If you had met Jeffrey, what advice would you give him? How would you help him?

6. Would you recommend *Maniac Magee* to another student? Why or why not?

7. Discuss Spinelli's statement in the introduction: "The history of a kid is one part fact, two parts legend, and three parts snowball. And if you want to know what it was like back when Maniac Magee roamed these parts, well, just run your hand under your movie seat and be very, very careful not to let the facts get mixed up with the truth."

8. Will you read more of Jerry Spinelli's books? Why or why not?

9. Did you have strong feelings while reading this book? If so, what did the author do to cause those feelings? If not, why not?

10. What makes Jerry Spinelli a unique and different author?

11. What questions would you like to ask Jerry Spinelli?

12. What was the funniest part of the story? What was the saddest part? What was the most exciting part?

13. What do you remember most about the story?

14. What picture did Jerry Spinelli leave in your mind?

15. What did *Maniac Magee* make you think about?

QUOTATIONS *Maniac Magee*

Discuss the significance of the following quotations.

1. "Talk! Talk, will ya! Talk! Talk! Talk!"

2. "Hi."

3. "Are you running away?"

4. "Books!"

5. "Where are you from? West End?"
   "No."
   "I know you're not from the East End."
   "I'm from Bridgeport."
   "Bridgeport? Over there? *That* Bridgeport?"
   "Yep."
   "Well, why aren't you there?"
   "It's where I'm from, not where I am."
   "Great. So where do you *live*?"
   "I don't know. . . maybe. . . here?"
   Maybe? *May*be you better go ask your mother and father if you live here or not."

6. "I'll bring it back. Honest! If it's the last thing I do. What's your address?"
   "Seven twenty-eight Sycamore. But *you* can't come there. You can't even be *here*."

7. "No! No! Please! Pleeeeeeeeese!"

8. "Who's that kid?"
   "What kid?" said Duke.
   "The kid next to you at the table."
   "I don't know. I thought Donald knew him."
   "I don't know him," said Donald. "I thought Dion knew him."
   "Never saw him," said Dion. "I figured he was Deidre's new boyfriend."
   "He's gone!"

9. "Get outta there, runt. This is a Little League record. You ain't in Little League."

10. "Don't stop till you're outta town, runt! Don't let me ever catch ya!"

11. "Kid's gotta be a maniac."
    "Yeah, reg'lar maniac."
    "Yeah."

12. "He's dead. "Let's get 'im."

13. "Wanna bite?"
    "You sure?"
    "Yeah, go ahead. Take a bite."
    "Thanks."

14. "You think you come down here and be bad? That what you think? "
    "No, I don't think I'm bad. I'm not saying I'm an angel, either. Not even real good. Somewhere in between, I guess."
    "Am I bad?"
    "I don't know. One minute you're yelling at me, the next minute you're giving me a bite of your candy bar."
    "Tell me I'm bad."
    "It's none of my business. If you're bad, let your mother or father tell you."

15. "I got a little brother and a little sister that crayon all over my books, and I got a dog that eats them and poops on them and that's just inside my own family, and I'm *not*--gonna have *nobody*--else--*messin'*--with my *books*! You under-*stand*?"

16. "Want to come to my house?"

17. "This is it."

18. "You're staying here."

19. "Never saw such a tub."

20. "You *have* eaten pizza before, haven't you?"

21. "Hallelujah! A-*men*!"

22. "You that Maniac?"
    "I'm Jeffrey. You know me."
    "Yeah, I know you all right. You'll be nothing but Jeffrey in here. But--out there, I don't know."

23. "I'm sorry. I love you . . . I love you."

24. "You move on now, Whitey. You pick up your gear and move on out. Time to go home now."

25. "What happens when we go over there? Black is black! White is white! The sheep lie not with the lion! The sheep knows his own! His own kind!"

26. ISHBELLY GO HOME

27. "Well, I'll tell you one thing, buddy boy. You better shut the door on your way out and lock it, because if I ever get my room back, I'm not giving it up again. So don't *ever* come crawling back around here. You *hear*?"

28. "Oh no! Oh no! It was my fault. I got careless. I left it in the living room. Anybody could look through the window and . . . and "

29. "Yo baby, we hear ya got a little pizza prize there. . . come on back . . . we missed ya . . . we been waitin' for ya. . . "

30. "Can we go somewhere and get some butterscotch Krimpets?"

31. "What about school?"
    "What about it?"
    "You gotta go. You're a kid. Ain't ya?"
    "I'm not going."
    "But you gotta go. Doncha? They'll make ya."
    "Not if they don't find me."
    "If you try to make me, I'll just start running."

32. "Them black people, they eat mashed potatoes, too?"

33. Wait--What did you want to grow up to be when you were a kid?"
    "A baseball player."

34. "I ain't got no stories."

35. "So, why don't you go ahead and teach me how to read?"

36. "Grayson? *Grayson*!"

37. "You know, you're taking the long way to Mexico. If you come back to Two Mills with me, I'll show you a shortcut."

38. "Well, well, the frog man. So what're you doing with my little brothers?"

39. "Soon's they start comin' in ---bam-bam-bam!"
"Who?"
"The enemy."
"Who's that?"
"Who do ya think?"

40. "I'm back."

41. "They like to revolt in the summer. Makes 'em itchy. They like to overrun the cities. This time we'll be ready."

42. "Get outta my house."
"Yeah, outta here."

43. "No? You wanna tell me why I ain't so bad, fish? Go ahead, fore I waste ya."
"Simple. You don't cross Hector. You stay over here, where it's safe. How bad would you be over there?"
"Guess that makes me badder than you."

44. "Let me know when it leaves."

45. "Yeah, bomb shelter."

46. "You suckered me. You soften me up with them Pick-peoples, then bring me here. What'd you think? I was gonna cry? Okay, I come over. I did it. It's done. And don't you be comin' 'round no more, ya hear me, fish? 'Cause you ain't only seen me *half* bad yet."

47. "I knew you wasn't scared."

48. "They say, 'Come on --*pleeeese*--if you *play* with us, we'll let you be white.' You *believe* that?"

49. "She wants to know, like, uh, why don't you come to our house?"
"I didn't say I didn't want to. It's just . . . I don't know . . . things happen . . . I can't . . . "

50. "Don't tell me *can't* I didn't come all the way out here in my nightshirt and my slippers and climb that fence and almost kill myself so I could hear you tell me *can't*."

LESSON SIXTEEN

Student Objectives
1. To extend the story by means of a project
2. To work cooperatively in a group

Note to the Teacher: The following projects may be used as a means of alternative assessment, for extra credit, or as an assessment in addition to the test.

Activity #1
Allow students to choose one of the following projects. Give them the class period to complete it. If students need more time, you can assign the project as homework or add another day onto the unit plan.

PROJECT IDEAS

1. Draw a book jacket that summarizes the story.

2. Write a critique of the book.

3. Make a timeline showing the important events from the story.

4. Make a diorama showing one of the scenes from the book.

5. Make clay models of the people and setting in the book.

6. Make puppets and write a puppet show to illustrate one scene from the story.

7. Write a radio or television commercial to advertise the book.

8. Design a poster to advertise the book.

9. Write a different ending to the story.

10. Make a comic book version of the story to share with younger readers.

11. Make a mobile showing the main character, secondary characters and setting.

13. Create a "Missing Person" poster describing Jeffrey.

14. Create a poster showing some of Maniac's feats.

15. Make a collage based on scenes from the book.

16. Write a new jump rope rhyme based on Maniac's feats.

17. Write another myth about Maniac.

18. Write a newspaper or television report about Maniac untying Cobble's Knot.

19. Collect the picture books that Grayson read. Read them aloud to the class.

20. Make a copy of the book *The Man Who Struck Out Willie Mays* that Jeffrey wrote for Grayson. Read it aloud to the class.

21. Collect some polka records. Learn to polka, or invite adults who can polka to visit the class and demonstrate. You might also find a video that teaches the polka, and show it to the class.

LESSON SEVENTEEN

Student Objective
    To review all of the vocabulary work done in this unit

VOCABULARY REVIEW ACTIVITIES

1. Divide your class into two teams and have an old-fashioned spelling or definition bee.

2. Give individuals or groups of students a *Maniac Magee* Vocabulary Word Search Puzzle. The person (group) to find all of the vocabulary words in the puzzle first wins.

3. Give students a *Maniac Magee* Vocabulary Word Search Puzzle without the word list. The person or group to find the most vocabulary words in the puzzle wins.

4. Put a *Maniac Magee* Vocabulary Crossword Puzzle onto a transparency on the overhead projector and do the puzzle together as a class.

5. Give students a *Maniac Magee* Vocabulary Matching Worksheet to do.

6. Use words from the word jumble page and have students spell them correctly.

7. Have students write a story in which they correctly use as many vocabulary words as possible. Have students read their compositions orally. Post the most original compositions on your bulletin board.

8. Have students work in teams and play charades with the vocabulary words.

9. Select a word of the day and encourage students to use it correctly in their writing and speaking vocabulary.

10. Have a contest to see which students can find the most vocabulary words used in other sources. You may want to have a bulletin board available so the students can write down their word, the sentence it was used in, and the source.

11. Assign a word to each student, or let them choose a word. Have them look up the origin of the word, the part of speech, definition, a synonym, and an antonym. Then have them write a sentence using the word. Have students present their information orally to the class, or have them design a word map on paper and display the papers.

LESSON EIGHTEEN

Objective
> To review the main ideas presented in *Maniac Magee*

Activity #1
> Choose one of the review games/activities included in the packet and spend your class period as outlined there.

Activity #2
> Remind students of the date for the Unit Test. Stress the review of the Study Guides and their class notes as a last minute, brush-up review for homework.

REVIEW GAMES / ACTIVITIES

1. Ask the class to make up a unit test for *Maniac Magee*. The test should have 4 sections: multiple choice, true/false, short answer and essay. Students may use 1/2 period to make the test, including a separate answer sheet, and then swap papers and use the other 1/2 class period to take a test a classmate has devised. (open book)

2. Take 1/2 period for students to make up true and false questions (including the answers). Collect the papers and divide the class into two teams. Draw a big tic-tac-toe board on the chalk board. Make one team X and one team O. Ask questions to each side, giving each student one turn. If the question is answered correctly, that student's team's letter (X or O) is placed in the box. If the answer is incorrect, no mark is placed in the box. The object is to get three marks in a row like tic-tac-toe. You may want to keep track of the number of games won for each team.

3. Take 1/2 period for students to make up questions (true/false and short answer). Collect the questions. Divide the class into two teams. You'll alternate asking questions to individual members of teams A & B (like in a spelling bee). The question keeps going from A to B until it is correctly answered, then a new question is asked. A correct answer does not allow the team to get another question. Correct answers are +2 points; incorrect answers are -1 point.

4. Allow students time to quiz each other (in pairs) from their study guides and class notes.

5. Give students a *Maniac Magee* crossword puzzle to complete.

6. Divide your class into two teams. Use the *Maniac Magee* crossword words with their letters jumbled as a word list. Student 1 from Team A faces off against Student 1 from Team B. You write the first jumbled word on the board. The first student (1A or 1B) to unscramble the word wins the chance for his/her team to score points. If 1A wins the jumble, go to student 2A and give him/her a clue. He/she must give you the correct word which matches that clue. If he/she does, Team A scores a point, and you give student 3A a clue for which you expect another correct response. Continue giving Team A clues until some team member makes an incorrect response. An incorrect response sends the game back to the jumbled-word face off, this time with students 2A and 2B. Instead of repeating giving clues to the first few students of each team, continue with the student after the one who gave the last incorrect response on the team.

7. Take on the persona of "The Answer Person." Allow students to ask any question about the book. Answer the questions, or tell students where to look in the book to find the answer.

8. Students may enjoy playing charades with events from the story. Select a student to start. Give him/her a card with a scene or event from the story. Allow the players to use their books to find the scene being described. The first person to guess each charade performs the next one.

9. Play a categories-type quiz game. (A master is included in this Unit Plan). Make an overhead transparency of the categories form. Divide the class into teams of three or four players each. Have each team Choose a recorder and a banker. Choose a team to go first. That team will choose a category and point amount. Ask the question to the entire class.(Use the Study Guide Quiz and Vocabulary questions.) Give the teams one minute to discuss the answer and write it down. Walk around the room and check the answers. Each team that answers correctly receives the points. (Incorrect answers are not penalized; they just don't receive any points). Cross out that square on the playing board. Play continues until all squares have been used. The winning team is the one with the most points. You can assign bonus points to any square or squares you choose.

10. Have individual students draw scenes from the book. Display the scenes and have the rest of the class look in their books to find the chapter or section that is being depicted. The first student to find the correct scene then displays his or her picture. When the game is over, collect the pictures and put them in a binder for students to look at during their free time.

NOTE: If students do not need the extra review, omit this lesson and go on to the test.

QUIZ GAME *Maniac Magee*

Chapters 1-11	Chapters 12-21	Chapters 22-32	Chapters 33-37	Chapters 38-46
100	100	100	100	100
200	200	200	200	200
300	300	300	300	300
400	400	400	400	400
500	500	500	500	500

LESSON NINETEEN

Student Objective
To demonstrate understanding of the main ideas and themes in *Maniac Magee*

Activity #1
Distribute the *Maniac Magee* Unit Tests. Go over the instructions in detail and allow the students the entire class period to complete the exam.

Activity #2
Collect all test papers and assigned books prior to the end of the class period.

NOTES ABOUT THE UNIT TESTS IN THIS UNIT:

There are 5 different unit tests which follow.

There are two short answer tests which are based primarily on facts from the novel. The answer key for short answer unit test 1 follows the student test. The answer key for short answer test 2 follows the student short answer unit test 2.

There is one advanced short answer unit test. It is based on the extra discussion questions. Use the matching key for short answer unit test 2 to check the matching section of the advanced short answer unit test. There is no key for the short answer questions. The answers will be based on the discussions you have had during class.

There are two multiple choice unit tests. Following the two unit tests, you will find an answer sheet on which students should mark their answers. The same answer sheet should be used for both tests; however, students' answers will be different for each test. Following the students' answer sheet for the multiple choice tests you will find your answer keys.

The short answer tests have a vocabulary section. You should choose 10 of the vocabulary words from this unit, read them orally and have the students write them down. Then, either have students write a definition or use the words in sentences. The second part of the vocabulary test is matching.

LESSON TWENTY

Objectives
1. To widen the breadth of students' knowledge about the topics discussed or touched upon in *Maniac Magee*
2. To check students' non-fiction assignments

Activity
Ask each student to give a brief oral report about the nonfiction work he/she read for the nonfiction assignment. Your criteria for evaluating this report will vary depending on the level of your students. You may wish for students to give a complete report without using notes of any kind, or you may want students to read directly from a written report, or you may want to do something in between these two extremes. Just make students aware of your criteria in ample time for them to prepare their reports.

Start with one student's report. After that, ask if anyone else in the class has read on a topic related to the first student's report. If no one has, choose another student at random. After each report, be sure to ask if anyone has a report related to the one just completed. That will help keep a continuity during the discussion of the reports.

UNIT TESTS

SHORT ANSWER UNIT TEST 1 *Maniac Magee*

I. <u>Matching/ Identify</u>

Directions: Place the letter of the matching definition on the blank line.

_____ 1. West End   A. white family that fed Maniac
_____ 2. Amanda   B. went to school because of Maniac
_____ 3. East End   C. where the whites lived
_____ 4. Mars Bar   D. went to a party with Maniac
_____ 5. Pickwell   E. black family who took Maniac in
_____ 6. Butterscotch Krimpets   F. where the blacks lived
_____ 7. Hester & Lester   G. liked to take baths with Maniac
_____ 8. Beale   H. Maniac was allergic to it
_____ 9. pizza   I. Maniac's favorite food
_____ 10. Russell & Piper   J. carried a suitcase full of books

II. <u>Short Answer</u>

1. Describe Maniac's early life. What was his real name? Whom did he live with, and why? What was his life there like? How long did he live there? How and when did he leave? Where did he end up?

2. How was Maniac blind? What did he think about skin color? How did he finally find out about skin color?

Short Answer Unit Test 1 *Maniac Magee*

3. Describe the time Maniac knew Grayson. Who was Grayson, and how did he meet Maniac? Where did Maniac live? What was special about Grayson's past? What did Maniac and Grayson do together? What happened to Grayson? What did Maniac do after that?

4. Describe the McNab house and family. What did Maniac do while he lived there?

5. Discuss the meaning of the following quotation: "Wanna bite?" "You sure?" "Yeah, go ahead. Take a bite." "Thanks."

Short Answer Unit Test 1 *Maniac Magee*

III. Fill-in-the-Blank

1. Maniac's real name was _____. He got the nickname because of some of the things he did.

2. One of the first things Maniac did was _____ from Brian Denehy, then punt the ball to James "Hands" Down. He did most of this with one hand, because he was carrying a book in the other.

3. Next, he rescued Arnold Jones from _____ back yard. Later, he went back and stayed in the yard for 10 minutes on a dare.

4. After that, Maniac joined the Little League game. John McNab threw a fastball that most of the other kids could not hit. When it looked like he was not going to be able to strike Maniac out, John threw a _____ at him. Maniac bunted it, and got a four-bagger.

5. The kids were surprised to see Maniac running on _____, because none of them were able to do it.

6. Maniac was very unusual because he lived with a _____ family, and he was _____. Some people did not like this.

7. Maniac was the only person who was able to _____. He won a large pizza a week for a year for doing this.

8. For a while, Maniac lived with the _____ at the zoo. The legend says he kissed the baby one.

9. Maniac won a footrace with _____.

10. At the end of the story, Maniac found a home. Then he felt _____.

Short Answer Unit Test 1 *Maniac Magee*

IV. <u>Essay</u>   What are the main conflicts in the story? How are they resolved?
.

Short Answer Unit Test 1 *Maniac Magee*

IV. Vocabulary Part 1

Listen to the vocabulary words and spell them. After you have spelled all the words, go back and write down the definitions.

WORD	DEFINITION
1. _____	_____
2. _____	_____
3. _____	_____
4. _____	_____
5. _____	_____
6. _____	_____
7. _____	_____
8. _____	_____
9. _____	_____
10. _____	_____

Vocabulary Part 2   Directions: Place the letter of the matching definition on the blank line.

____ 1. apparently   A. disorderly
____ 2. chaotic   B. ridiculous
____ 3. contortions   C. skill in deception
____ 4. cunning   D. indifferent to pain or pleasure
____ 5. ecstatic   E. shrunk back in fear
____ 6. flinched   F. easily understood
____ 7. grouse   G. uproar; confusion
____ 8. ludicrous   H. overjoyed
____ 9. pandemonium   I. twisting and bending out of shape
____ 10. stoic   J. complain; grumble

ANSWER KEY SHORT ANSWER UNIT TEST 1 *Maniac Magee*

I. Matching/ Identify

C	1.	West End	A.	white family that fed Maniac
J	2.	Amanda	B.	went to school because of Maniac
F	3.	East End	C.	where the whites lived
D	4.	Mars Bar	D.	went to a party with Maniac
A	5.	Pickwell	E.	black family who took Maniac in
I	6.	Butterscotch Krimpets	F.	where the blacks lived
G	7.	Hester & Lester	G.	liked to take baths with Maniac
E	8.	Beale	H.	Maniac was allergic to it
H	9.	pizza	I.	Maniac's favorite food
B	10.	Russell & Piper	J.	carried a suitcase full of books

II. Short Answer

1. Describe Maniac's early life. What was his real name? Whom did he live with, and why? What was his life there like? How long did he live there? How and when did he leave? Where did he end up?

   Maniac's real name was Jeffrey Lionel Magee. He lived with his Aunt Dot and Uncle Dan. When he was three, his parents were killed when the trolley they were on crashed into the river. His aunt and uncle did not speak to each other. They had two of everything. Maniac spent part of his time with each one of them. He lived like that for eight years. The night of the school musical, Maniac was singing with the chorus. When the singing stopped, he was still screaming "Talk! Talk, will ya!" He ran down from the risers and kept on going. He went to Two Mills, across the river from Bridgeport. It took him a year to get there.

2. How was Maniac blind? What did he think about skin color? How did he finally find out about skin color?

   He didn't see that big kids didn't like little ones showing them up. He didn't see that the big kids didn't like having another big kid (Hands Down) laughing at them while the little one showed them up. He didn't see that some kids didn't like him because he was different, especially a different color. Manic could not understand the fuss about skin color. He didn't think he was white: he was a combination of different shades and colors. He discovered skin color while the kids were playing in the water from the fire hydrant. An old black man called him "Whitey" and told him to go back to his own kind.

3. Describe the time Maniac knew Grayson. Who was Grayson, and how did he meet Maniac? Where did Maniac live? What was special about Grayson's past? What did Maniac and Grayson do together? What happened to Grayson? What did Maniac do after that?

   Grayson was the attendant at the Elmwood Park Zoo. He found Maniac lying on the ground outside the buffalo pen. He took Maniac to the empty band shell. Grayson got some food, and then Maniac told him his story. Grayson took Maniac to the YMCA, and got him a shower. Then he took Maniac shopping and bought him new clothes. Manic discovered that Grayson had been a pitcher in the minor leagues. In the mornings, Maniac helped Grayson repair fences around the park. In the afternoons, Grayson gave Maniac baseball instructions. Then Maniac taught Grayson to read. Grayson died a few days after Christmas. After that, Maniac thought about dying himself, but eventually went to live with the McNab family.

4. Describe the McNab house and family. What did Maniac do while he lived there?

   It was smelly and dirty. There were cans, bottles, and garbage all over. There was a partially dissected bird on the kitchen table. The only foods in the refrigerator were beer and mustard. Maniac made a deal with Russell and Piper, the two younger boys. He met all of the challenges they thought up. In return, they went to school and did their work.

5. Discuss the meaning of the following quotation: "Wanna bite?" "You sure?" "Yeah, go ahead. Take a bite." "Thanks."

   Maniac had just run into the East End. He was not aware that the blacks and white lived in different parts of town, and he was in the black section. He met Mars Bar Thompson, the local tough guy. Mars Bar offered Maniac a bite of a candy bar. Maniac bit right over the spot where Mars Bar had eaten. It was unthinkable because Mars Bar was black and Maniac was white.

II. Fill-in-the-Blank

1. Maniac's real name was **Jeffrey Lionel Magee.** He got the nickname because of some of the things he did.

2. One of the first things Maniac did was **intercept a pass** from Brian Denehy, then punt the ball to James "Hands" Down. He did most of this with one hand, because he was carrying a book in the other.

3. Next, he rescued Arnold Jones from **Finsterwald's** back yard. Later, he went back and stayed in the yard for 10 minutes on a dare.

4. After that, Maniac joined the Little League game. John McNab threw a fastball that most of the other kids could not hit. When it looked like he was not going to be able to strike Maniac out, John threw a **frogball** at him. Maniac bunted it, and got a four-bagger.

5. The kids were surprised to see Maniac running on **the train rail** because none of them were able to do it.

6. Maniac was very unusual because he lived with a **black** family, although he was **white**. Some people did not like this.

7. Maniac was the only person who was able to **untie Cobble's Knot**. He won a large pizza a week for a year for doing this.

8. For a while, Maniac lived with the **buffalo/bison** at the zoo. The legend says he kissed the baby one.

9. Maniac won a footrace with **Mars Bar Thompson**.

10. At the end of the story, Maniac found a home. Then he felt **content**.

IV. Vocabulary Part 1 Choose ten vocabulary words to dictate for this section of the test.

Vocabulary Part 2

F	1.	apparently	A.	disorderly
A	2.	chaotic	B.	ridiculous
I	3.	contortions	C.	skill in deception
C	4.	cunning	D.	indifferent to pain or pleasure
H	5.	ecstatic	E.	shrunk back in fear
E	6.	flinched	F.	easily understood
J	7.	grouse	G.	uproar; confusion
B	8.	ludicrous	H.	overjoyed
G	9.	pandemonium	I.	twisting and bending out of shape
D	10.	stoic	J.	complain; grumble

SHORT ANSWER UNIT TEST 2 *Maniac Magee*

I. <u>Matching/Identify</u>   Directions: Place the letter of the matching definition on the blank line.

____ 1. Beale   A. East End family Maniac lived with
____ 2. McNab   B. took care of Maniac at the band shell
____ 3. Pickwell   C. where Jeffrey's aunt and uncle lived
____ 4. Cobble   D. where Jeffrey ended up
____ 5. Grayson   E. the zoo where Jeffrey lived
____ 6. Bridgeport   F. family that often fed Maniac at dinner time
____ 7. Two Mills   G. street that divided the East and West ends
____ 8. Hector   H. owner of the famous knot and store
____ 9. Hollidaysburg   I. where Jeffrey was born
____ 10. Elmwood   J. West End family Maniac lived with

II. <u>Short Answer</u>

1. How was Maniac blind? What did he think about skin color? How did he finally find out about skin color?

2. How did Jeffrey get the name "Maniac?" What were some of the things he did?

Short Answer Unit Test 2 *Maniac Magee*

3. What was Jeffrey afraid of losing, and why?

4. Describe the party at the McNab house. Who attended with Maniac? What happened at the party? What did Maniac learn about himself?

5. Discuss the importance of the following quotation: "Don't tell me *can't*. I didn't come all the way out here in my nightshirt and my slippers and climb that fence and almost kill myself so I could hear you tell me *can't*."

Short Answer Unit Test 2 *Maniac Magee*

III. Fill-in-the Blank

1. After Maniac left the Beales' home, he lived in the buffalo pen at the zoo. Grayson, the park attendant, found him lying outside the pen one morning. He took Maniac to the _____.

2. After Grayson got some food for Maniac, the two of them went to the _____, where Grayson lived. Maniac took a shower. Then Grayson took Maniac shopping and bought him some _____.

3. Maniac said he wanted to stay in the _____ at the _____.

4. Grayson asked Maniac about school. Maniac said he would _____ if Grayson tried to make him go to school.

5. Grayson asked a lot of questions about the black people who lived in the East End. One of the things he asked about was (choose any one) _____ _____.

6. Maniac discovered that Grayson had been a _____ when he was younger.

7. Maniac taught Grayson how to _____.

8. Maniac painted the address _____ on the door.

9. Maniac and Grayson enjoyed their time together. One morning a few days after Christmas, Maniac discovered that Grayson was _____.

10. After that, Maniac ran all around the area. He slept at the zoo or in abandoned cars. Then he went to Valley Forge and stayed in one of the old Revolutionary War cabins. He was waiting for _____.

Short Answer Unit Test 2 *Maniac Magee*

IV. Essay

What is Jerry Spinelli saying about prejudice? Is it effective? Give examples from the story to support your answer.

Short Answer Unit Test 2 *Maniac Magee*

V. Vocabulary Part 1

Listen to the vocabulary words and spell them. After you have spelled all the words, go back and write down the definitions.

WORD	DEFINITION
1. _____	_____
2. _____	_____
3. _____	_____
4. _____	_____
5. _____	_____
6. _____	_____
7. _____	_____
8. _____	_____
9. _____	_____
10. _____	_____

Vocabulary Part 2 Directions: Place the letter of the matching definition on the blank line.

_____ 1. exuberance   A. having a very bad reputation
_____ 2. infamous   B. violently excited
_____ 3. minutely   C. flat
_____ 4. prone   D. a miserable, unfortunate person
_____ 5. pry   E. speaking in a violent manner
_____ 6. ranting   F. enthusiasm
_____ 7. rickety   G. unspecified
_____ 8. seething   H. to force open or up
_____ 9. vague   I. concerned with small details
_____ 10. wretch   J. shaky

ANSWER KEY SHORT ANSWER UNIT TEST 2 *Maniac Magee*

I. <u>Matching/Identify</u>

Note: Use this key for the Advanced Short Answer Matching Test.

A	1.	Beale	A.	East End family Maniac lived with
J	2.	McNab	B.	took care of Maniac at the band shell
F	3.	Pickwell	C.	where Jeffrey's aunt and uncle lived
H	4.	Cobble	D.	where Jeffrey ended up
B	5.	Grayson	E.	the zoo where Jeffrey lived
I	6.	Bridgeport	F.	family that often fed Maniac at dinner time
D	7.	Two Mills	G.	street that divided the East and West ends
G	8.	Hector	H.	owner of the famous knot and store
C	9.	Hollidaysburg	I.	where Jeffrey was born
E	10.	Elmwood	J.	West End family Maniac lived with

II. <u>Short Answer</u>

1. How was Maniac blind? What did he think about skin color? How did he finally find out about skin color?

    He didn't see that big kids didn't like little ones showing them up. He didn't see that the big kids didn't like having another big kid (Hands Down) laughing at them while the little one showed them up. He didn't see that some kids didn't like him because he was different, especially a different color. Manic could not understand the fuss about skin color. He didn't think he was white: he was a combination of different shades and colors. He discovered skin color while the kids were playing in the water from the fire hydrant. An old black man called him "Whitey" and told him to go back to his own kind.

2. How did Jeffrey get the name "Maniac?" What were some of the things he did?

He got the name because of the things he did. Spinelli says that probably people started talking and said things like: "Kid's gotta be a maniac." "Yeah, a reg'lar maniac."

One of the first things Maniac did was **intercept a pass** from Brian Denehy, then punt the ball to James "Hands" Down. He did most of this with one hand, because he was carrying a book in the other. Next, he rescued Arnold Jones from **Finsterwald's** back yard. Later, he went back and stayed in the yard for 10 minutes on a dare.

After that, Maniac joined the Little League game. John McNab threw a fastball that most of the other kids could not hit. When it looked like he was not going to be able to strike Maniac out, John threw a **frogball** at him. Maniac bunted it, and got a four-bagger.

The kids were surprised to see Maniac running on **the train rail** because none of them were able to do it.

Maniac was very unusual because he lived with a **black** family, although he was **white**. Some people did not like this.

Maniac was the only person who was able to **untie Cobble's Knot**. He won a large pizza a week for a year for doing this.

The jump rope rhyme said he kissed a bull, but it was probably the baby bison at the zoo.

3. What was Jeffrey afraid of losing, and why?

He was afraid of losing his name. It was all he had left from his parents and his former life.

4. Describe the party at the McNab house. Who attended with Maniac? What happened at the party? What did Maniac learn about himself?

Maniac went to Piper's party and took a guest. It was Mars Bar Thompson. Maniac thought it was a good idea because the blacks and the whites did not know much about each other.

He took a compass. He told Piper he could have the compass if both boys went to school every day until the school year was finished.

George McNab went upstairs and told the others to let him know when Mars Bar left. He referred to Mars Bar as "it."

One of the Cobras jumped through the hole in the ceiling. He landed behind Mars Bar. Mars Bar wanted to charge the boy, but Maniac held him back. John McNab started teasing Mars Bar. They traded insults. Maniac dragged Mars Bar out of the house and down the street.

After it was over, Manic wondered why he had taken Mars Bar with him. He wondered if he had expected a miracle. Then he realized a he was proud of Mars Bar for not showing his fear.

5. Discuss the importance of the following quotation: "Don't tell me *can't*. I didn't come all the way out here in my nightshirt and my slippers and climb that fence and almost kill myself so I could hear you tell me *can't*."

    This quote is at the very end of the book. Amanda and Mars Bar went to the buffalo pen at the zoo to get Maniac. Amanda wanted Maniac to go home with her, but he refused. She climbed into the pen. They argued, and Maniac finally agreed to go with her.

III. Fill-in-the Blank

1. After Maniac left the Beales' home, he lived in the buffalo pen at the zoo. Grayson, the park attendant, found him lying outside the pen one morning. He took Maniac to the **band shell**.

2. After Grayson got some food for Maniac, the two of them went to the **YMCA**, where Grayson lived. Maniac took a shower. Then Grayson took Maniac shopping and bought him some **clothes**.

3. Maniac said he wanted to stay in the locker **room** at the **band shell at the zoo**.

4. Grayson asked Maniac about school. Maniac said he would **run away** if Grayson tried to make him go to school.

5. Grayson asked a lot of questions about the black people who lived in the East End. One of the things he asked about was (choose any one) **what they ate, if they brushed their teeth, if they drank out of the same glass in the bathroom**.

6. Maniac discovered that Grayson had been a **minor league baseball pitcher when** he was younger.

7. Maniac taught Grayson how to **read**.

8. Maniac painted the address **101 Band Shell Boulevard** on the door.

9. Maniac and Grayson enjoyed their time together. One morning a few days after Christmas, Maniac discovered that Grayson was **dead**

10. After that, Maniac ran all around the area. He slept at the zoo or in abandoned cars. Then he went to Valley Forge and stayed in one of the old Revolutionary War cabins. He was waiting for **death**

V. Vocabulary Part 1 Choose ten of the vocabulary words to dictate for this part of the test.

Vocabulary Part 2

F	1.	exuberance	A.	having a very bad reputation
A	2.	infamous	B.	violently excited
I	3.	minutely	C.	flat
C	4.	prone	D.	a miserable, unfortunate person
H	5.	pry	E.	speaking in a violent manner
E	6.	ranting	F.	enthusiasm
J	7.	rickety	G.	unspecified
B	8.	seething	H.	to force open or up
G	9.	vague	I.	concerned with small details
D	10.	wretch	J.	shaky

ADVANCED SHORT ANSWER UNIT TEST *Maniac Magee*

I. <u>Matching/Identify</u>   Directions: Place the letter of the matching definition on the blank line.

____ 1. Beale   A. East End family Maniac lived with
____ 2. McNab   B. took care of Maniac at the band shell
____ 3. Pickwell   C. where Jeffrey's aunt and uncle lived
____ 4. Cobble   D. where Jeffrey ended up
____ 5. Grayson   E. the zoo where Jeffrey lived
____ 6. Bridgeport   F. family that often fed Maniac at dinner time
____ 7. Two Mills   G. street that divided the East and West ends
____ 8. Hector   H. owner of the famous knot and store
____ 9. Hollidaysburg I. where Jeffrey was born
____ 10. Elmwood   J. West End family Maniac lived with

II. Short Answer

1. Complete a story map for Maniac Magee. Use this space or the other side of the paper.

2. The introduction says that it's hard to know what's true and what's a myth. Which parts of the story do you think could be true? Which could be myths?

Advanced Short Answer Unit Test *Maniac Magee*

3. What is Jerry Spinelli saying about prejudice? Is the way he says it effective?

4. How did Jeffrey change over the course of the novel?

5. Which of Maniac's relationships (with Grayson, Amanda, Mars Bar, the McNab boys) was most fully developed? Use examples to support your answer.

Advanced Short Answer Unit Test *Maniac Magee*

III. Quotations

Discuss the importance of the following quotations. Tell who said it, to whom the speaker was talking, and what event was going on at the time.

1. "Talk! Talk, will ya! Talk! Talk! Talk!"

2. "I'll bring it back. Honest! If it's the last thing I do. What's your address?"
   "Seven twenty-eight Sycamore. But *you* can't come there. You can't even be *here*."

3. "You that Maniac?"
   "I'm Jeffrey. You know me."
   "Yeah, I know you all right. You'll be nothing but Jeffrey in here. But--out there, I don't know."

4. "Wait--What did you want to grow up to be when you were a kid?"
   "A baseball player."

5. "Don't tell me *can't* I didn't come all the way out here in my nightshirt and my slippers and climb that fence and almost kill myself so I could hear you tell me *can't*."

Advanced Short Answer Unit Test *Maniac Magee*

IV. Vocabulary

Listen to the words and write them down. After you have written down all of the words, write a paragraph in which you use all of the words. The paragraph must in some way relate to *Maniac Magee*.

1. _____   6. _____
2. _____   7. _____
3. _____   8. _____
4. _____   9. _____
5. _____   10. _____

MULTIPLE CHOICE UNIT TEST 1 *Maniac Magee*

I. <u>Matching/ Identify</u>   Directions: Place the letter of the matching definition on the blank line.

___ 1.	West End	A.	white family that fed Maniac
___ 2.	Amanda	B.	went to school because of Maniac
___ 3.	East End	C.	where the McNab family lived
___ 4.	Mars Bar	D.	went to a party with Maniac
___ 5.	Pickwell	E.	black family who took Maniac in
___ 6.	Butterscotch Krimpets	F.	where the Beale family lived
___ 7.	Hester & Lester	G.	liked to take baths with Maniac
___ 8.	Beale	H.	Maniac was allergic to it
___ 9.	pizza	I.	Maniac's favorite food
___ 10.	Russell & Piper	J.	carried a suitcase full of books

II. <u>Multiple Choice</u> Directions: Circle the letter next to the correct answer.

1. Which of the following does **not** describe Maniac's early life?
    A. Maniac lived with his older sister and her husband.
    B. When he was three, his parents were killed when the trolley they were on crashed into the river.
    C. His relatives did not speak to each other. They had two of everything. Maniac spent part of his time with each one of them.
    D. He lived with them for eight years.

2. Which statement is **true**?
    A. The blacks lived in the North End and the whites lived in the South End.
    B. The blacks lived in Westport and the whites lived in Eastport.
    C. The blacks lived in the South Side and the whites lived in the North Side.
    D. The blacks lived in the East End, and the whites lived in the West End.

3. After dinner at the Pickwell house, Jeffrey ran somewhere that the other kids had only walked. Where was it?
    A. Jeffrey ran up the side of the mountain in his bare feet.
    B. Jeffrey ran along the roofs of the houses on Hector Street.
    C. Jeffrey ran the entire length of the P&W trolley route in one hour.
    D. Jeffrey ran on the railroad tracks with a book in his hand.

Multiple Choice Unit Test 1 *Maniac Magee*

4. True or False: The people in the town were all taking about Jeffrey and his deeds. Someone probably said, "Kid's gotta be a maniac." Others agreed. Since they didn't know his real name, they started calling him Maniac.
    A. True
    B. False

5. Mars Bar and some friends followed Maniac and backed him against a wall. What happened **next**?
    A. A policeman saw them and stopped the fight.
    B. A woman in the neighborhood hit Mars Bar and the others with her broom and chased them away.
    C. Amanda found them. She kicked Mars Bar, Then she invited Manic to her house.
    D. Maniac jumped over the wall and ran away.

6. Which of the following did **not** happen in the Beale household after Maniac moved in?
    A. Hester and Lester started eating vegetables for dinner every night.
    B. Hester and Lester stopped crayoning on the walls and furniture.
    C. Hester and Lester began taking baths willingly.
    D. Hester and Lester stopped damaging Amanda's books.

7. What happened to Maniac while the children were playing in the fire hydrant water?
    A. One of the older boys tried to drown Maniac.
    B. The police stopped and asked him what he was doing in the East End.
    C. He slipped and broke his leg.
    D. An old man called him "Whitey" and told him to go back to his own kind.

8. What did Grayson ask Maniac to do?
    A. Grayson asked Maniac to play baseball with him.
    B. Grayson asked Maniac to teach him to read.
    C. Grayson asked Maniac to call his aunt and uncle and tell them he was fine.
    D. Grayson asked Maniac to call him Grandpa.

9. When did Maniac think about his parents being killed?
    A. He thought about it every time he visited Grayson's tomb at the cemetery.
    B. He thought about it every night before he went to sleep.
    C. He thought about it whenever he took a bath in the lake in the park.
    D. He thought about it whenever he crossed the bridge over the Schuylkill River.

Multiple Choice Unit Test 1 *Maniac Magee*

10. How did Maniac feel at the end of the book?
    A. He was scared.
    B. He was sad.
    C. He was content.
    D. He was tired.

Multiple Choice Unit Test 1 *Maniac Magee*

III. <u>Quotations</u> Directions: Write the letter of the second part of the quotation on the line.

___ 1. "I'll bring it back. Honest! If it's the last thing I do. What's your address?"
___ 2. "Am I bad?"
___ 3. "You move on now, Whitey."
___ 4. "You that Maniac?"
___ 5. "No? You wanna tell me why I ain't so bad, fish? Go ahead, fore I waste ya."
"Simple. You don't cross Hector. You stay over here, where it's safe. How bad would you be over there? Guess that makes me badder than you."
___ 6. "Let me know . . .
___ 7. "So, why don't you go ahead. . .
___ 8. "You suckered me. You soften me up with them Pick-peoples, then bring me here. What'd you think? I was gonna cry?
___ 9. "I knew you. . .
___ 10. "Don't tell me *can't* . . .

===

A. "You pick up your gear and move on out. Time to go home now."
B. wasn't scared."
C. "Simple. You don't cross Hector. You stay over here, where it's safe. How bad would you be over there? Guess that makes me badder than you."
D. when it leaves."
E. "Seven twenty-eight Sycamore. But *you* can't come there. You can't even be *here*."
F. and teach me how to read?"
G. I didn't come all the way out here in my nightshirt and my slippers and climb that fence and almost kill myself so I could hear you tell me *can't*."
H. "I'm Jeffrey. You know me."
"Yeah, I know you all right. You'll be nothing but Jeffrey in here. But--out there, I don't know."
I. Okay, I come over. I did it. It's done. And don't you be comin' 'round no more, ya hear me, fish? 'Cause you ain't only seen me *half* bad yet."
J. "I don't know. One minute you're yelling at me, the next minute you're giving me a bite of your candy bar."

Multiple Choice Unit Test 1 *Maniac Magee*

IV. Vocabulary Part 1   Directions: Place the letter of the matching definition on the blank line.

____ 1.	apparently	A.	disorderly
____ 2.	chaotic	B.	ridiculous
____ 3.	contortions	C.	skill in deception
____ 4.	cunning	D.	indifferent to pain or pleasure
____ 5.	ecstatic	E.	shrunk back in fear
____ 6.	flinched	F.	easily understood
____ 7.	grouse	G.	uproar; confusion
____ 8.	ludicrous	H.	overjoyed
____ 9.	pandemonium	I.	twisting and bending out of shape
____ 10.	stoic	J.	complain; grumble

Vocabulary Part 2   Directions: Circle the letter next to the word that matches the definition.

11. **jeering**
    a. lunging
    b. seething
    c. scoffing
    d. lurching

12. **speaking in a violent manner**
    a. accurate
    b. grizzled
    c. ranting
    d. halted

13. **developing and hatching**
    a. scoffing
    b. incubating
    c. bellowing
    d. converged

14. **looking into the future**
    a. flinched
    b. cringed
    c. incubating
    d. foresight

15. **instant; immediate**
    a. accurate
    b. apparently
    c. sleazy
    d. prompt

16. **stopped**
    a. halted
    b. hoisted
    c. languished
    d. wrenched

17. **deadly**
    a. finicky
    b. fatal
    c. infamous
    d. ludicrous

18. **powerful motivations or impulses**
    a. grates
    b. digits
    c. conclusions
    d. instincts

19. **a guide or guard**
    a. commotion
    b. escort
    c. gauntlet
    d. quiver

20. **to make known**
    a. reveal
    b. expire
    c. quiver
    d. obvious

MULTIPLE CHOICE UNIT TEST 2 *Maniac Magee*

I. <u>Matching/Identify</u> Directions: Place the letter of the matching definition on the blank line.

___ 1.	Beale	A.	East End family Maniac lived with
___ 2.	McNab	B.	took care of Maniac at the band shell
___ 3.	Pickwell	C.	where Jeffrey's aunt and uncle lived
___ 4.	Cobble	D.	where Jeffrey ended up
___ 5.	Grayson	E.	the zoo where Jeffrey lived
___ 6.	Bridgeport	F.	family that often fed Maniac at dinner time
___ 7.	Two Mills	G.	street that divided the East and West ends
___ 8.	Hector	H.	owner of the famous knot and store
___ 9.	Hollidaysburg	I.	where Jeffrey was born
___ 10.	Elmwood	J.	West End family Maniac lived with

II. <u>Multiple Choice</u>

Directions: Circle the letter next to the correct answer.

1. Which of the following does **not** describe Maniac's early life?
    A. Maniac lived with his older sister and her husband.
    B. When he was three, his parents were killed when the trolley they were on crashed into the river.
    C. His relatives did not speak to each other. They had two of everything. Maniac spent part of his time with each one of them.
    D. He lived with them for eight years.

2. A group of high school kids dumped Arnold Jones into Finsterwald's back yard and ran off. Arnold got the "finsterwallies", or violent shakes. What did Maniac do?
    A. He threw two of the high school boys over the fence and made them bring Arnold out.
    B. He rang Finsterwald's doorbell and asked if he could have the key to unlock the gate.
    C. Maniac carried Arnold to the front step. Then Maniac sat on the steps and started reading.
    D. Maniac helped Arnold climb over the back fence. Then the two of them went to the drugstore for sodas.

Multiple Choice Unit Test 2 *Maniac Magee*

3. How did he like Amanda's book?
    A. He didn't like it, but did not remember where she lived to take it back.
    B. He liked the pictures, but could not read the words.
    C. He liked it but was bored after he read it once.
    D. He was so fascinated that he read it over and over.

4. True or False: Maniac thought he was pure white and his friends in the East End were pure black.
    A. True
    B. False

5. What was Jeffrey afraid of losing?
    A. He was afraid of losing the Beale family and his home, because he was white.
    B. He was afraid of losing Amanda, who was his only friend.
    C. He was afraid of losing his name, the only thing he had left from his parents.
    D. He was afraid of losing his freedom by staying with the Beale family.

6. Describe the way Maniac left town after he untied Cobble's Knot.
    A. He ran on the P&W track.
    B. Mr. Beale drove him.
    C. He rode Amanda's bicycle.
    D. He walked down the middle of Hector Street.

7. How did Maniac react when Grayson read his first book?
    A. He jumped up and down and said "Yippee!"
    B. He drew a gold star and pinned it on Grayson's shirt.
    C. He said, "A-men."
    D. He whistled and clapped.

8. What did Maniac do when he discovered Grayson was dead?
    A. He told the zookeeper right away.
    B. He ran out of the room and locked it. He stayed outside for two days.
    C He held Grayson's hand, talked to him and read aloud all his books.
    D. He cried and screamed. He shook Grayson and yelled. "Wake up."

Multiple Choice Unit Test 2 *Maniac Magee*

9. True or False: The McNabs were building a pillbox. They thought the blacks in the East End were going to revolt, and they wanted to be ready for it.
    A. True
    B. False

10. How did Maniac feel at the end of the book?
    A. He was scared.
    B. He was sad.
    C. He was content.
    D. He was tired.

Multiple Choice Unit Test 2 *Maniac Magee*

III. Quotations

Directions: Write the letter of the second part of the quotation on the line.

___ 1. "I got a little brother and a little sister that crayon all over my books, and I got a dog that eats them and pops on them and that's just inside my own family. . .
___ 2. "Never saw. . .
___ 3. "Wait. What did you want to grow up to be when you were a kid?"
___ 4. "Them black people. . .
___ 5. "You know, you're taking the long way to Mexico. . .
___ 6. "You that Maniac?"
___ 7. "What happens when we go over there? . . .
___ 8. "Am I bad?"
___ 9. "She wants to know, like, uh, why don't you come to our house?"
___ 10. "I knew you . . .

==

A. such a tub."
B. If you come back to Two Mills with me, I'll show you a shortcut."
C. Black is black. White is white. The sheep lie not with the lion! The sheep knows his own! His own kind!"
D. they eat mashed potatoes, too?"
E. "I'm Jeffrey. You know me."
F. "I don't know. One minute you're yelling at me,, the next minute you're giving me a bite of your candy bar."
G. and I'm *not* gonna have *nobody* ---else--*messin'* ---with my *books*! You under--*stand*?"
H. "I didn't say I didn't want to. It's just. . . I don't know. . . things happen . . . I can't."
I. wasn't scared."
J. "A baseball player."

Multiple Choice Unit Test 2 *Maniac Magee*

Vocabulary Part 1 Directions: Place the letter of the matching definition on the blank line.

____	1.	exuberance	A.	having a very bad reputation
____	2.	infamous	B.	violently excited
____	3.	minutely	C.	flat
____	4.	prone	D.	a miserable, unfortunate person
____	5.	pry	E.	speaking in a violent manner
____	6.	ranting	F.	enthusiasm
____	7.	rickety	G.	unspecified
____	8.	seething	H.	to force open or up
____	9.	vague	I.	concerned with small details
____	10.	wretch	J.	shaky

Vocabulary Part 2 Directions: Underline the word that matches the definition.

11. **to make known**
    a. reveal
    b. expire
    c. quiver
    d. obvious

12. **instant; immediate**
    a. accurate
    b. apparently
    c. sleazy
    d. prompt

13. **end results**
    a. compliments
    b. instincts
    c. conclusions
    d. reprisals

14. **looking into the future**
    a. flinched
    b. cringed
    c. incubating
    d. foresight

15. **a guide or guard**
    a. commotion
    b. escort
    c. gauntlet
    d. quiver

16. **moving in a clumsy way**
    a. scowling
    b. contortions
    c. chaotic
    d. blundering

17. **deadly**
    a. finicky
    b. fatal
    c. infamous
    d. ludicrous

18. **developing and hatching**
    a. scoffing
    b. incubating
    c. bellowing
    d. converged

19. **stopped**
    a. halted
    b. hoisted
    c. languished
    d. wrenched

20. **one who is against another**
    a. mammoth
    b. random
    c. opponent
    d. pursuers

ANSWER SHEET Multiple Choice Unit Tests *Maniac Magee*

I. Matching	III. Quotations	IV. Vocabulary
1. ____	1. ____	1. ____
2. ____	2. ____	2. ____
3. ____	3. ____	3. ____
4. ____	4. ____	4. ____
5. ____	5. ____	5. ____
6. ____	6. ____	6. ____
7. ____	7. ____	7. ____
8. ____	8. ____	8. ____
9. ____	9. ____	9. ____
10. ____	10. ____	10. ____
		11. ____
		12. ____

II. Multiple Choice

1. (A) (B) (C) (D)   13. ____
2. (A) (B) (C) (D)   14. ____
3. (A) (B) (C) (D)   15. ____
4. (A) (B) (C) (D)   16. ____
5. (A) (B) (C) (D)   17. ____
6. (A) (B) (C) (D)   18. ____
7. (A) (B) (C) (D)   19. ____
8. (A) (B) (C) (D)   20. ____
9. (A) (B) (C) (D)
10. (A) (B) (C) (D)

ANSWER SHEET KEY Multiple Choice Unit Test 1 *Maniac Magee*

I. Matching	III. Quotations	IV. Vocabulary
1. C	1. E	1. F
2. J	2. J	2. A
3. F	3. A	3. I
4. D	4. H	4. C
5. A	5. C	5. H
6. I	6. D	6. E
7. G	7. F	7. J
8. E	8. I	8. B
9. H	9. B	9. G
10. B	10. G	10. D
		11. C
		12. C
II. Multiple Choice		13. B
1. ( ) (B) (C) (D)		14. D
2. (A) (B) (C) ( )		15. D
3. (A) (B) (C) ( )		16. A
4. ( ) (B) (C) (D)		17. B
5. (A) ( ) (C) (D)		18. D
6. ( ) (B) (C) (D)		19. B
7. (A) (B) (C) ( )		20. A
8. (A) ( ) (C) (D)		
9. (A) (B) (C) ( )		
10. (A) (B) ( ) (D)		

ANSWER SHEET KEY Multiple Choice Unit Test 2 *Maniac Magee*

I. Matching		III. Quotations		IV. Vocabulary	
1.	A	1.	G	1.	F
2.	J	2.	A	2.	A
3.	F	3.	J	3.	I
4.	H	4.	D	4.	C
5.	B	5.	B	5.	H
6.	I	6.	E	6.	E
7.	D	7.	C	7.	J
8.	G	8.	F	8.	B
9.	C	9.	H	9.	G
10.	E	10.	I	10.	D
				11.	A
				12.	D
				13.	C
				14.	D
				15.	B
				16.	D
				17.	B
				18.	B
				19.	A
				20.	C

II. Multiple Choice

1. ( ) (B) (C) (D)
2. (A) (B) ( ) (D)
3. (A) (B) (C) ( )
4. (A) ( ) (C) (D)
5. (A) (B) ( ) (D)
6. (A) (B) (C) ( )
7. (A) (B) ( ) (D)
8. (A) (B) ( ) (D)
9. ( ) (B) (C) (D)
10. (A) (B) ( ) (D)

UNIT RESOURCES

BULLETIN BOARD IDEAS *Maniac Magee*

1. Save one corner of the board for the best of students' *Maniac Magee* writing assignments. You may want to use background maps of the Philadelphia area and suburbs to represent the setting of the novel.

2. Take one of the word search puzzles from the extra activities packet and with a marker copy it over in a large size on the bulletin board. Write the clue words to find to one side. Invite students prior to and after class to find the words and circle them on the bulletin board.

3. Have students find or draw pictures that they think resemble the people in the book.

4. Invite students to help make an interactive bulletin board quiz. Give each student a half-sheet of paper (about 4"x5') folded in half so that it can open. On the outside flap, have each student write a description of one of the characters in the text. On the inside, they will write the name of the character. You can staple or tack these papers to the bulletin board so that the students can read the descriptions and lift the flaps to find the answers.

5. Collect pictures to represent the setting of the novel--the northwestern suburbs of Philadelphia, Pa. especially the Norristown and Valley Forge areas. Include photos of the elevated trains.

   Make a display of pictures of student-drawn book jackets and artwork from the novel.

7. Display articles about the novel and/or the author, Jerry Spinelli.
8. Have students design postcards depicting the settings of the book.

9. Display a large map of Pennsylvania and have students mark the route that Maniac took as he ran from Hollidaysburg to Two Mills.

10. Make a large map of the zoo and label the places where Maniac lived.

EXTRA ACTIVITIES *Maniac Magee*

One of the difficulties in teaching a novel is that all students don't read at the same speed. One student who likes to read may take the book home and finish it in a day or two. Sometimes a few students finish the in-class assignments early. The problem, then, is finding suitable extra activities for students.

One thing that helps is to keep a little library in the classroom. For this unit on *Maniac Magee* you might check out from the school or public library other books by Jerry Spinelli.. Several journals have critiques of Spinelli's works. Some of the students may enjoy reading these and responding either in writing or in discussion groups.

Your students who have reading difficulties, or speak English as a second language may benefit from listening to all or part of the book on tape. Record the tape yourself, or purchase a commercially made tape.

Other things you may keep on hand are word search puzzles. Several puzzles relating directly to *Maniac Magee* are included in the unit. Feel free to duplicate them.

Some students may like to draw. You might devise a contest or allow some extra-credit grade for students who draw characters or scenes from *Maniac Magee*. Note, too, that if the students do not want to keep their drawings you may pick up some extra bulletin board materials this way. If you have a contest and you supply the prize. You could, possibly, make the drawing itself a non-refundable entry fee.

Have maps, a globe, and travel brochures on hand for easy reference. Travel agencies and automobile clubs are good sources for these materials. You may also want to contact the Bureau of Travel Marketing, Pennsylvania Dept. of Commerce, 453 Forum Bldg. Harrisburg, PA, 17120 (800) 847-4872 for information about the state.

The pages which follow contain games, puzzles, and worksheets. The keys, when appropriate, immediately follow the puzzle or worksheet. There are two main groups of activities: one group for the unit; that is, generally relating to the *Maniac Magee* text, and another group of activities related strictly to the *Maniac Magee* vocabulary.

Directions for the games, puzzles, and worksheets are self-explanatory. The object here is to provide you with extra materials you may use in any way you choose.

MORE ACTIVITIES *MANIAC MAGEE*

1. Dramatize one of the incidents from the story. Write dialog for the characters. Create simple costumes and props.

2. Design a book cover (front and back and inside flaps) for *Maniac Magee.*

3. Design a bulletin board (ready to be put up; not just sketched) for *Maniac Magee.*

4. Invite a story teller to tell one or more stories related to *Maniac Magee* to the class.

5. Design and produce a talk show. Choose one of the story incidents as the topic. The host will interview the various characters. Students should make up the questions they want the host to ask the characters.

6. Invite students who have read other books by Jerry Spinelli to present booktalks to the class.

7. Invite students who have read a biography of Jerry Spinelli to tell the class about his life.

8. Invite someone who has lived in or visited the Philadelphia/Norristown area book to speak to the class.

9. Invite someone who has worked with runaway children/teens to talk to the class.

10. Invite someone who learned to read as an adult, or who teaches adults to read, to talk to the class.

11. Hold small group discussions related to topics in the book. Assign a recorder and a speaker for each group. Have the speaker from each group make a report to the class.

12. Write a sequel to the story, telling about Maniac's other adventures.

13. Re-write the story in a comic book format. Give a copy of the comic book to a lower grade class.

14. Choose a quote from the book and illustrate it. Display the quotes on the bulletin board.

WORD SEARCH - Maniac Magee

```
J S N R P R O T E C T O R S R O N I M A
M E C R U L T V V G N Y N T Z P X R Z M
J U F R A S N S O F E A K M V X E Z D H
G G L F E F S R W L T P M J V P I P G Z
Z E F L R A N E E K N M X A I P P O T F
N U O H I E M K L X O S S P N M M L T V
B T P R A G Y C S L C Y Y D X D E K E X
P H I H G N A I Q W C N N A B E A A L D
L O L S S E D N R A L J A J R V M S M C
P M L T J N Y S M V R M H H J N J T W S
G P B N D A C O N F E T T I G N O L O S
R S O A H M R M S N D K E C T N H L O Q
A O X N M E L C A R I M B A N D N A D T
Y N S O K P C R R Y H S B A M N A B M Y
S M T S Y N I T B W S L F M T B C G Y C
O J K N N K O T O H S L R K B H M O T F
N G L O V E C T C R L I B R A R Y R O G
H P Z C A L N R O H Z M I I R G A F D N
D Q N S I A E E U J E A S M L I Q C T K
Q A T O R T S S L S N R N P N D J L R P
C C N D S R D T D V A L L E Y U R E A D
X E Y E A C R L Q R Z D X T F M R W S B
L H H M G R L E S T E R E S H P F Z H D
```

AMANDA	CRUSADE	HESTER	MINORS	RUSSELL
ARNOLD	DAN	HYDRANT	MIRACLE	SCREAM
BAND	DOT	JEFFREY	MULLIGAN	SNICKERS
BATH	DUMP	JOHN	NAME	SYCAMORE
BETHANY	EAST	KNOT	PILLBOX	THOMPSON
BRIAN	ELMWOOD	KRIMPETS	PIPER	THREE
BUFFALO	FROGBALL	LESTER	PITCHER	TRAIN
COBRAS	GEORGE	LIBRARY	PIZZA	TRASH
CONFETTI	GLOVE	LIONEL	POLKAS	TRESTLE
CONSONANTS	GRAYSON	MARS	PROTECTORS	VALLEY
CONTENT	HANDS	MAYS	RAN	VOWELS
COULD	HECTOR	MILLS	READ	YMCA

WORD SEARCH ANSWER KEY - Maniac Magee

AMANDA	CRUSADE	HESTER	MINORS	RUSSELL
ARNOLD	DAN	HYDRANT	MIRACLE	SCREAM
BAND	DOT	JEFFREY	MULLIGAN	SNICKERS
BATH	DUMP	JOHN	NAME	SYCAMORE
BETHANY	EAST	KNOT	PILLBOX	THOMPSON
BRIAN	ELMWOOD	KRIMPETS	PIPER	THREE
BUFFALO	FROGBALL	LESTER	PITCHER	TRAIN
COBRAS	GEORGE	LIBRARY	PIZZA	TRASH
CONFETTI	GLOVE	LIONEL	POLKAS	TRESTLE
CONSONANTS	GRAYSON	MARS	PROTECTORS	VALLEY
CONTENT	HANDS	MAYS	RAN	VOWELS
COULD	HECTOR	MILLS	READ	YMCA

165

CROSSWORD *Maniac Magee*

CROSSWORD CLUES *Maniac Magee*

ACROSS

1 Scary house in East End
7 She had a suitcase full of books
12 Taught Maniac to play baseball
13 Maniac read it and won
15 End where the blacks lived
17 Grayson lived there when he met Maniac
18 Grayson's Christmas present to Maniac
20 McNabs were building one in their living room
22 Jeffrey's middle name
23 Maniac walked barefoot through it
27 Jeffrey was afraid of losing it
29 Maniac taught Grayson to do it
31 Where Jeffrey was born
35 First book Grayson read: The Little Engine That ___
37 Jeffrey did it during the concert
39 Amanda's 4 year old sister
40 Star quarterback
41 Amanda said she was changing Mars Bar's name to this

DOWN

1 Maniac logged the world's first one
2 Russell was stuck on it
3 High school kids put him in Finsterwald's yard
4 Uncle ___ didn't talk to his wife
5 Receiver doing a fly pattern: ___ down
6 The trolley car fell off the track and into this river
8 Aunt ___ hated her husband
9 Maniac lived there when he knew Grayson: ___ shell
10 Made of string with lots of contortions: cobble's ___
11 Maniac was allergic to it
14 Stuck on the trolley trestle
15 Where Maniac slept at first: ___ Park Zoo
16 Age when Jeffrey became an orphan
18 Called Mars Bar "It"
19 Maniac went to ___ Forge to wait for death
20 Grayson's position
21 Amanda's 3 year old brother
24 Where Grayson played baseball
25 McNab's group of friends
26 Maniac took one every night with Hester and Lester
28 The book Maniac wrote for Grayson: The Man Who Struck Out Willie ___
30 Invited Maniac to his birthday party
32 Music Maniac and Grayson listened to
33 Mrs. Beale didn't want Maniac using this kind of talk in her house
34 Street that divided East and West Ends
36 Went to the McNab house with Maniac: ___ Bar
38 Jeffrey did this early in the morning, all over town

CROSSWORD ANSWER KEY *Maniac Magee*

				F	I	N	S	T	E	R	W	A	L	D		H					
S				R				R				R		A	M	A	N	D	A		
C			B		E		K		N			N			O				P		
H		G	R	A	Y	S	O	N				O			D		T	R	A	I	N
U		B		N		T		O		L			E	A	S	T		U		Z	
Y	M	C	A		D		L		T		D		L		H		S		Z		
L		L			E						M		R		S		A				
K	G	L	O	V	E						W		E		E						
I	E		A			P	I	L	L	B	O	X		E		L					
L	I	O	N	E	L		T		E		O					L					
L	R		L		I		S		D	U	M	P									
	G		E		E		C		T		I										
C	E		Y		H		E		B		N	A	M	E							
O					E		R	E	A	D		O		A						P	
B	R	I	D	G	E	P	O	R	T			T		R		Y		H		I	
R					O		R		H			H		S		S		E		P	
A			C	O	U	L	D		A		M							C		E	
S				K		S	C	R	E	A	M		H	E	S	T	E	R			
		B	R	I	A	N		H		A						O					
			S			N		S	N	I	C	K	E	R	S						

MATCHING QUIZ/WORKSHEET 1 - Maniac Magee

___ 1. LIBRARY   A. Maniac taught Grayson to do it
___ 2. CONTENT   B. The trolley car fell off the track and into this river
___ 3. RUSSELL   C. Maniac's real first name
___ 4. KNOT   D. Maniac kissed a baby one
___ 5. CONSONANTS   E. Maniac walked barefoot through it
___ 6. MIRACLE   F. How Maniac felt at the end of the story
___ 7. HANDS   G. Jeffrey kept his room clean
___ 8. DUMP   H. Maniac raced it and won
___ 9. ELMWOOD   I. Maniac went to ___ Forge to wait for death
___ 10. TRAIN   J. Made of string with lots of contortions: cobble's ___
___ 11. CRUSADE   K. Easy for Grayson to learn
___ 12. HOLLIDAYSBURG   L. Maniac was allergic to it
___ 13. JEFFREY   M. Aunt ___ hated her husband
___ 14. BATH   N. Title of book Maniac borrowed from Amanda: Children's ___
___ 15. COULD   O. Someone used Amanda's book to make it
___ 16. PIZZA   P. Where Maniac's aunt and uncle lived
___ 17. CONFETTI   Q. Went to the McNab house with Maniac: ___ Bar
___ 18. VOWELS   R. Stuck on the trolley trestle
___ 19. VALLEY   S. Where Maniac slept at first: ___ Park Zoo
___ 20. BAND   T. Receiver doing a fly pattern: ___ down
___ 21. BUFFALO   U. These were hard for Grayson to learn
___ 22. DOT   V. First book Grayson read: The Little Engine That ___
___ 23. READ   W. Amanda said Maniac could not get this card without an address
___ 24. MARS   X. Maniac lived there when he knew Grayson: ___ shell
___ 25. SCHUYLKILL   Y. Maniac took one every night with Hester and Lester

KEY: MATCHING QUIZ/WORKSHEET 1 - Maniac Magee

W - 1.	LIBRARY	A. Maniac taught Grayson to do it
F - 2.	CONTENT	B. The trolley car fell off the track and into this river
R - 3.	RUSSELL	C. Maniac's real first name
J - 4.	KNOT	D. Maniac kissed a baby one
K - 5.	CONSONANTS	E. Maniac walked barefoot through it
G - 6.	MIRACLE	F. How Maniac felt at the end of the story
T - 7.	HANDS	G. Jeffrey kept his room clean
E - 8.	DUMP	H. Maniac raced it and won
S - 9.	ELMWOOD	I. Maniac went to ___ Forge to wait for death
H - 10.	TRAIN	J. Made of string with lots of contortions: cobble's ___
N - 11.	CRUSADE	K. Easy for Grayson to learn
P - 12.	HOLLIDAYSBURG	L. Maniac was allergic to it
C - 13.	JEFFREY	M. Aunt ___ hated her husband
Y - 14.	BATH	N. Title of book Maniac borrowed from Amanda: Children's ___
V - 15.	COULD	O. Someone used Amanda's book to make it
L - 16.	PIZZA	P. Where Maniac's aunt and uncle lived
O - 17.	CONFETTI	Q. Went to the McNab house with Maniac: ___ Bar
U - 18.	VOWELS	R. Stuck on the trolley trestle
I - 19.	VALLEY	S. Where Maniac slept at first: ___ Park Zoo
X - 20.	BAND	T. Receiver doing a fly pattern: ___ down
D - 21.	BUFFALO	U. These were hard for Grayson to learn
M - 22.	DOT	V. First book Grayson read: The Little Engine That ___
A - 23.	READ	W. Amanda said Maniac could not get this card without an address
Q - 24.	MARS	X. Maniac lived there when he knew Grayson: ___ shell
B - 25.	SCHUYLKILL	Y. Maniac took one every night with Hester and Lester

MATCHING QUIZ/WORKSHEET 2 - Maniac Magee

___ 1. HYDRANT   A. Jeffrey did this early in the morning, all over town

___ 2. FINSTERWALD   B. McNabs were building one in their living room

___ 3. LESTER   C. Grayson's favorite book: Mike ___ and His Steam Shovel

___ 4. CRUSADE   D. Jeffrey kept his room clean

___ 5. GEORGE   E. Maniac liked to eat butterscotch ones

___ 6. HESTER   F. Kids had a swimming party there: fire ___

___ 7. PROTECTORS   G. Amanda's 3 year old brother

___ 8. MIRACLE   H. Invited Maniac to his birthday party

___ 9. TRAIN   I. Age when Jeffrey became an orphan

___ 10. FROGBALL   J. Maniac kissed a baby one

___ 11. AMANDA   K. Maniac logged the world's first one

___ 12. RAN   L. Called Mars Bar IT

___ 13. BAND   M. Title of book Maniac borrowed from Amanda: Children's ___

___ 14. BUFFALO   N. McNab's group of friends

___ 15. THREE   O. Uncle ___ didn't talk to his wife

___ 16. MULLIGAN   P. The trolley car fell off the track and into this river

___ 17. COBRAS   Q. Maniac slept on them: chest ___

___ 18. PIPER   R. Maniac raced it and won

___ 19. MINORS   S. Scary house in East End

___ 20. PILLBOX   T. Maniac lived there when he knew Grayson: ___ shell

___ 21. KRIMPETS   U. Where Grayson played baseball

___ 22. LIBRARY   V. She had a suitcase full of books

___ 23. JEFFREY   W. Amanda's 4 year old sister

___ 24. SCHUYLKILL   X. Maniac's real first name

___ 25. DAN   Y. Amanda said Maniac could not get this card without an address

KEY: MATCHING QUIZ/WORKSHEET 2 - Maniac Magee

F - 1. HYDRANT	A. Jeffrey did this early in the morning, all over town
S - 2. FINSTERWALD	B. McNabs were building one in their living room
G - 3. LESTER	C. Grayson's favorite book: Mike ___ and His Steam Shovel
M - 4. CRUSADE	D. Jeffrey kept his room clean
L - 5. GEORGE	E. Maniac liked to eat butterscotch ones
W - 6. HESTER	F. Kids had a swimming party there: fire ___
Q - 7. PROTECTORS	G. Amanda's 3 year old brother
D - 8. MIRACLE	H. Invited Maniac to his birthday party
R - 9. TRAIN	I. Age when Jeffrey became an orphan
K - 10. FROGBALL	J. Maniac kissed a baby one
V - 11. AMANDA	K. Maniac logged the world's first one
A - 12. RAN	L. Called Mars Bar IT
T - 13. BAND	M. Title of book Maniac borrowed from Amanda: Children's ___
J - 14. BUFFALO	N. McNab's group of friends
I - 15. THREE	O. Uncle __ didn't talk to his wife
C - 16. MULLIGAN	P. The trolley car fell off the track and into this river
N - 17. COBRAS	Q. Maniac slept on them: chest ___
H - 18. PIPER	R. Maniac raced it and won
U - 19. MINORS	S. Scary house in East End
B - 20. PILLBOX	T. Maniac lived there when he knew Grayson: ___ shell
E - 21. KRIMPETS	U. Where Grayson played baseball
Y - 22. LIBRARY	V. She had a suitcase full of books
X - 23. JEFFREY	W. Amanda's 4 year old sister
P - 24. SCHUYLKILL	X. Maniac's real first name
O - 25. DAN	Y. Amanda said Maniac could not get this card without an address

JUGGLE LETTER REVIEW GAME CLUE SHEET 1 - Mainac Magee

1. RHDNAYT = 1. _____
   Kids had a swimming party there: fire ___

2. LOEINL = 2. _____
   Jeffrey's middle name

3. UCLDO = 3. _____
   First book Grayson read: The Little Engine That ___

4. YROSANG = 4. _____
   Taught Maniac to play baseball

5. NNETTOC = 5. _____
   How Maniac felt at the end of the story

6. WMOLODE = 6. _____
   Where Maniac slept at first: ___ Park Zoo

7. RCKSSNIE = 7. _____
   Amanda said she was changing Mars Bar's name to this

8. ADAANM = 8. _____
   She had a suitcase full of books

9. SAET = 9. _____
   End where the blacks lived

10. DMPU =10. _____
    Maniac walked barefoot through it

11. ADNHS =11. _____
    Receiver doing a fly pattern: ___ down

12. NICTTFEO =12. _____
    Someone used Amanda's book to make it

13. EOLVG =13. _____
    Grayson's Christmas present to Maniac

14. NONCNATSSO =14. _____
    Easy for Grayson to learn

15. CRASME =15. _____
    Jeffrey did it during the concert

16. ORTCTPROES =16. _____
   Maniac slept on them: chest ___

17. KCLUSLYILH =17. _____
   The trolley car fell off the track and into this river

18. URSSLLE =18. _____
   Stuck on the trolley trestle

19. RYJEFEF =19. _____
   Maniac's real first name

20. OPNHTSMO =20. _____
   Mars Bar's last name

21. BDGTREOPIR =21. _____
   Where Jeffrey was born

22. ESLTRE =22. _____
   Amanda's 3 year old brother

23. DAN =23. _____
   Uncle ___ didn't talk to his wife

24. OTD =24. _____
   Aunt ___ hated her husband

25. CEILARM =25. _____
   Jeffrey kept his room clean

26. SKPALO =26. _____
   Music Maniac and Grayson listened to

27. REESLTT =27. _____
   Russell was stuck on it

28. ILMSL =28. _____
   Where Jeffrey ended up: Two ___

29. EUDARCS =29. _____
   Title of book Maniac borrowed from Amanda: Children's ___

30. ZAPZI =30. _____
   Maniac was allergic to it

31. NERDWIAFSTL =31. _____
   Scary house in East End

KEY: JUGGLE LETTER REVIEW GAME CLUE SHEET 1 - Mainac Magee

1. RHDNAYT = 1. HYDRANT
Kids had a swimming party there: fire ___

2. LOEINL = 2. LIONEL
Jeffrey's middle name

3. UCLDO = 3. COULD
First book Grayson read: The Little Engine That ___

4. YROSANG = 4. GRAYSON
Taught Maniac to play baseball

5. NNETTOC = 5. CONTENT
How Maniac felt at the end of the story

6. WMOLODE = 6. ELMWOOD
Where Maniac slept at first: ___ Park Zoo

7. RCKSSNIE = 7. SNICKERS
Amanda said she was changing Mars Bar's name to this

8. ADAANM = 8. AMANDA
She had a suitcase full of books

9. SAET = 9. EAST
End where the blacks lived

10. DMPU =10. DUMP
Maniac walked barefoot through it

11. ADNHS =11. HANDS
Receiver doing a fly pattern: ___ down

12. NICTTFEO =12. CONFETTI
Someone used Amanda's book to make it

13. EOLVG =13. GLOVE
Grayson's Christmas present to Maniac

14. NONCNATSSO =14. CONSONANTS
Easy for Grayson to learn

15. CRASME =15. SCREAM
Jeffrey did it during the concert

16. ORTCTPROES =16. PROTECTORS
Maniac slept on them: chest ___

17. KCLUSLYILH =17. SCHUYLKILL
The trolley car fell off the track and into this river

18. URSSLLE =18. RUSSELL
Stuck on the trolley trestle

19. RYJEFEF =19. JEFFREY
Maniac's real first name

20. OPNHTSMO =20. THOMPSON
Mars Bar's last name

21. BDGTREOPIR =21. BRIDGEPORT
Where Jeffrey was born

22. ESLTRE =22. LESTER
Amanda's 3 year old brother

23. DAN =23. DAN
Uncle ___ didn't talk to his wife

24. OTD =24. DOT
Aunt ___ hated her husband

25. CEILARM =25. MIRACLE
Jeffrey kept his room clean

26. SKPALO =26. POLKAS
Music Maniac and Grayson listened to

27. REESLTT =27. TRESTLE
Russell was stuck on it

28. ILMSL =28. MILLS
Where Jeffrey ended up: Two ___

29. EUDARCS =29. CRUSADE
Title of book Maniac borrowed from Amanda: Children's ___

30. ZAPZI =30. PIZZA
Maniac was allergic to it

31. NERDWIAFSTL =31. FINSTERWALD
Scary house in East End

JUGGLE LETTER REVIEW GAME CLUE SHEET 2 - Mainac Magee

1. OUFABFL = 1. _____
   Maniac kissed a baby one

2. LDLYSHGBURIAO = 2. _____
   Where Maniac's aunt and uncle lived

3. OCEHTR = 3. _____
   Street that divided the East and West Ends

4. HTREE = 4. _____
   Age when Jeffrey became an orphan

5. PEIPR = 5. _____
   Invited Maniac to his birthday party

6. SMAR = 6. _____
   Went to the McNab house with Maniac: ___ Bar

7. ANYEHBT = 7. _____
   Church where Manic went with the Beales

8. EROGGE = 8. _____
   Called Mars Bar IT

9. HTAB = 9. _____
   Maniac took one every night with Hester and Lester

10. ARN =10. _____
    Jeffrey did this early in the morning, all over town

11. SBOARC =11. _____
    McNab's group of friends

12. AMSY =12. _____
    The book Maniac wrote for Grayson: The Man Who Struck Out Willie ___

13. HITRCPE =13. _____
    Grayson's position

14. LARGOLFB =14. _____
    Maniac logged the world's first one

15. ALMLNGIU =15. _____
    Grayson's favorite book: Mike ___ and His Steam Shovel

16. ACEECLIPNOYD =16. _____
Maniac got up early to read it

17. RIYBALR =17. _____
Amanda said Maniac could not get this card without an address

18. DABN =18. _____
Maniac lived there when he knew Grayson: ___ shell

19. NDRLOA =19. _____
High school kids put him in Finsterwald's yard

20. NRISMO =20. _____
Where Grayson played baseball

21. KLLSWCPEI =21. _____
Maniac and Mars Bar ate dinner with them

22. BLIPOLX =22. _____
McNabs were building one in their living room

23. SHREET =23. _____
Amanda's 4 year old sister

24. JHON =24. _____
Largest player in the Little League

25. AYMC =25. _____
Grayson lived there when he met Maniac

26. ARTHS =26. _____
Mrs. Beale didn't want Maniac using this kind of talk in her house

27. AERD =27. _____
Maniac taught Grayson to do it

28. NMEA =28. _____
Jeffrey was afraid of losing it

29. RABIN =29. _____
Star quarterback

30. YLEVLA =30. _____
Maniac went to ___ Forge to wait for death

31. EOLVWS =31. _____
These were hard for Grayson to learn

KEY: JUGGLE LETTER REVIEW GAME CLUE SHEET 2 - Mainac Magee

1. OUFABFL = 1. BUFFALO
   Maniac kissed a baby one

2. LDLYSHGBURIAO = 2. HOLLIDAYSBURG
   Where Maniac's aunt and uncle lived

3. OCEHTR = 3. HECTOR
   Street that divided the East and West Ends

4. HTREE = 4. THREE
   Age when Jeffrey became an orphan

5. PEIPR = 5. PIPER
   Invited Maniac to his birthday party

6. SMAR = 6. MARS
   Went to the McNab house with Maniac: ___ Bar

7. ANYEHBT = 7. BETHANY
   Church where Manic went with the Beales

8. EROGGE = 8. GEORGE
   Called Mars Bar IT

9. HTAB = 9. BATH
   Maniac took one every night with Hester and Lester

10. ARN = 10. RAN
    Jeffrey did this early in the morning, all over town

11. SBOARC = 11. COBRAS
    McNab's group of friends

12. AMSY = 12. MAYS
    The book Maniac wrote for Grayson: The Man Who Struck Out Willie ___

13. HITRCPE = 13. PITCHER
    Grayson's position

14. LARGOLFB = 14. FROGBALL
    Maniac logged the world's first one

15. ALMLNGIU = 15. MULLIGAN
    Grayson's favorite book: Mike ___ and His Steam Shovel

16. ACEECLIPNOYD =16. ENCYCLOPEDIA
Maniac got up early to read it

17. RIYBALR =17. LIBRARY
Amanda said Maniac could not get this card without an address

18. DABN =18. BAND
Maniac lived there when he knew Grayson: ___ shell

19. NDRLOA =19. ARNOLD
High school kids put him in Finsterwald's yard

20. NRISMO =20. MINORS
Where Grayson played baseball

21. KLLSWCPEI =21. PICKWELLS
Maniac and Mars Bar ate dinner with them

22. BLIPOLX =22. PILLBOX
McNabs were building one in their living room

23. SHREET =23. HESTER
Amanda's 4 year old sister

24. JHON =24. JOHN
Largest player in the Little League

25. AYMC =25. YMCA
Grayson lived there when he met Maniac

26. ARTHS =26. TRASH
Mrs. Beale didn't want Maniac using this kind of talk in her house

27. AERD =27. READ
Maniac taught Grayson to do it

28. NMEA =28. NAME
Jeffrey was afraid of losing it

29. RABIN =29. BRIAN
Star quarterback

30. YLEVLA =30. VALLEY
Maniac went to ___ Forge to wait for death

31. EOLVWS =31. VOWELS
These were hard for Grayson to learn

VOCABULARY RESOURCES

VOCABULARY WORD SEARCH - Maniac Magee

```
E X H A U S T I O N P U R S U E R S D L
Q C L E N C H E D R C I T A T S C E A L
K O F S U O L I R E P G A U N T L E T M
C N P R H W G N N V W Q D D W D V L R J
X V A B E L L O W I N G E G K E O L D Z
G E N V G I S J N U B I R S R T H M E J
W R D S G N T C G Q K I I K E L V I N N
S G E X C G U G V O Z E P K P A A L I X
T E M D B B N Q O Z X L X F R H C L F G
O D O V A I N R L U E Z E R I G A U N B
I R N T N F E E B D T N Y R S T N S O M
C R I N G E D E M M A R C H A O T I C F
Q N U C J C R S X X R N E F L N N O C L
G C M V K A M F Q D U P G L S D T N A V
O L S S N E F D P E C L R L U P L I I X
B U P C E L T I K T C V O O E C J N N B
V N E R O E U Y N S A M U Z N D T F A G
I G E N Y F T R Z I D W S T F E D A M J
O I R S D R F H C O C I E L B N N M N M
U N N A C U B I I H Y K G Y E N M O J T
S G E X T O R T N N I W Y I V A G U E M
G K C Z W E R E S G G N K W T C Z S N R
P R O M P T S T C S U R G E D S H Y S Q
```

ACCURATE	ENDURE	HALTED	PRONE	SCOFFING
BELLOWING	ESCORT	HOISTED	PRY	SCOWLING
CHAOTIC	EXHAUSTION	ILLUSION	PURSUERS	SEETHING
CLENCHED	EXPIRED	INCUBATING	QUIVER	SLEAZY
CONFINED	EXTORT	INFAMOUS	RANDOM	STOIC
CONVERGED	EXUBERANCE	LUNGING	RANTING	STUNNED
CRAMMED	FATAL	LURCHING	RELUCTANT	SURGED
CRINGED	FINICKY	MANIAC	REPRISALS	VACANT
CUNNING	GAUNTLET	OBVIOUS	REVEAL	VAGUE
DANGLED	GRATES	PANDEMONIUM	RICKETY	
DIGITS	GRIZZLED	PERILOUS	ROOKIE	
ECSTATIC	GROUSE	PROMPT	SCANNED	

VOCABULARY WORD SEARCH ANSWER KEY - Maniac Mage

ACCURATE	ENDURE	HALTED	PRONE	SCOFFING
BELLOWING	ESCORT	HOISTED	PRY	SCOWLING
CHAOTIC	EXHAUSTION	ILLUSION	PURSUERS	SEETHING
CLENCHED	EXPIRED	INCUBATING	QUIVER	SLEAZY
CONFINED	EXTORT	INFAMOUS	RANDOM	STOIC
CONVERGED	EXUBERANCE	LUNGING	RANTING	STUNNED
CRAMMED	FATAL	LURCHING	RELUCTANT	SURGED
CRINGED	FINICKY	MANIAC	REPRISALS	VACANT
CUNNING	GAUNTLET	OBVIOUS	REVEAL	VAGUE
DANGLED	GRATES	PANDEMONIUM	RICKETY	
DIGITS	GRIZZLED	PERILOUS	ROOKIE	
ECSTATIC	GROUSE	PROMPT	SCANNED	

VOCABULARY CROSSWORD *Maniac Magee*

VOCABULARY CROSSWORD CLUES *Maniac Magee*

ACROSS
 3 Crowded; packed
 6 To shake with a slight movement
 9 Disorderly
11 Apparent; observable
14 To bear with tolerance
17 Flat
18 Fantasy; false belief
20 Hung loosely
22 Parallel bars for blocking an opening
26 Exactly correct
28 Streaked with gray
30 To force open or up
33 To get by threats
34 Aloneness
35 Shabby and dirty
36 Having skill in deception

DOWN
 1 Deadly
 2 Indifferent to pain or pleasure
 4 Make known
 5 Overjoyed
 7 Unspecified; unclear
 8 Having no pattern or purpose
 9 Grasped tightly
10 Limited
12 One against another
13 Yelling
15 Gloom; bleakness
16 A first year player
19 Moved like waves
21 Easily understood
23 A guide or guard
24 Winced; recoiled
25 Moving in a clumsy way
27 Disturbance
29 Number symbols
31 Stopped
32 Complain; grumble

VOCABULARY CROSSWORD ANSWER KEY *Maniac Magee*

```
. . F . S . . . C R A M M E D . . . Q U I V E R
C H A O T I C . E . . . . C . . . . . . A . A N
L . T . O B V I O U S . . S . . . . . . G . N D
E . A . I . N E P T . . B . . . . . . . U . D O
N . L . C . F A P A . E N D U R E . . . . . . M
C . . . I . I L O T . L E O . . . . . . . . . .
H . . P R O N E . N . I L L U S I O N . . . . .
E . . . E . S . . E . C . O . . . K . . . . . .
D A N G L E D . . U . N . W . . L . I . . . . .
. P . . . . . G R A T E S . I . A . E . . . . .
. P . . C . . G . . S . . . N . T . B . . . . .
. A C C U R A T E . . . C . G R I Z Z L E D . .
. R . . I . . D . . . . O . . . O . U . . . . I
. E . . N . . . . . P R Y . H . N . N . . . . G
. N . . G . . . . G . T . . A . . . D . . . . I
. T . . . E X T O R T . S O L I T U D E . . . T
. L . . . . D . . . O . . . T . . . . . . R . S
. Y . . . . . . . . U . S L E A Z Y . . . I . .
. . . . . . . . . . S . . . D . . . . . . N . .
C U N N I N G . . . E . . . . . . . . . . G . .
```

VOCABULARY WORKSHEET 1 - Mainac Magee

___ 1. CRAMMED   A. Farfetched
___ 2. RICKETY   B. Weakened; faded
___ 3. LUDICROUS   C. Hung loosely
___ 4. CONVERGED   D. Jeering
___ 5. SCOFFING   E. Having a very bad reputation
___ 6. MAMMOTH   F. Moving forward suddenly
___ 7. HALTED   G. Flat
___ 8. SEETHING   H. Aloneness
___ 9. BLUNDERING   I. Parallel bars for blocking an opening
___10. GRATES   J. Followers trying to overtake; chasers
___11. LUNGING   K. Shaky
___12. DANGLED   L. Fantasy; false belief
___13. PURSUERS   M. Gigantic; enomous
___14. LANGUISHED   N. Violently excited
___15. SURGED   O. Developing and hatching
___16. STOIC   P. Came together
___17. WRENCHED   Q. Twisted
___18. PRY   R. Moving in a clumsy way
___19. GROUSE   S. Indifferent to pain or pleasure
___20. ILLUSION   T. Stopped
___21. SOLITUDE   U. Ridiculous
___22. INFAMOUS   V. Moved like waves
___23. PRONE   W. Crowded; packed
___24. PREPOSTEROUS   X. To force open or up
___25. INCUBATING   Y. Complain; grumble

KEY: VOCABULARY WORKSHEET 1 - Mainac Magee

W	1. CRAMMED	A.	Farfetched
K	2. RICKETY	B.	Weakened; faded
U	3. LUDICROUS	C.	Hung loosely
P	4. CONVERGED	D.	Jeering
D	5. SCOFFING	E.	Having a very bad reputation
M	6. MAMMOTH	F.	Moving forward suddenly
T	7. HALTED	G.	Flat
N	8. SEETHING	H.	Aloneness
R	9. BLUNDERING	I.	Parallel bars for blocking an opening
I	10. GRATES	J.	Followers trying to overtake; chasers
F	11. LUNGING	K.	Shaky
C	12. DANGLED	L.	Fantasy; false belief
J	13. PURSUERS	M.	Gigantic; enomous
B	14. LANGUISHED	N.	Violently excited
V	15. SURGED	O.	Developing and hatching
S	16. STOIC	P.	Came together
Q	17. WRENCHED	Q.	Twisted
X	18. PRY	R.	Moving in a clumsy way
Y	19. GROUSE	S.	Indifferent to pain or pleasure
L	20. ILLUSION	T.	Stopped
H	21. SOLITUDE	U.	Ridiculous
E	22. INFAMOUS	V.	Moved like waves
G	23. PRONE	W.	Crowded; packed
A	24. PREPOSTEROUS	X.	To force open or up
O	25. INCUBATING	Y.	Complain; grumble

VOCABULARY WORKSHEET 2 - Mainac Magee

___ 1. EXTORT   A. Disturbance
___ 2. PERILOUS   B. To get by threats
___ 3. BLUNDERING   C. Having no pattern or purpose
___ 4. ECSTATIC   D. Hung loosely
___ 5. OBVIOUS   E. Gigantic; enomous
___ 6. CONTORTIONS   F. To force open or up
___ 7. ILLUSION   G. Fantasy; false belief
___ 8. WRETCH   H. A miserable, unfortunate person
___ 9. PRY   I. Twisted
___10. RICKETY   J. Dangerous
___11. HALTED   K. Disorderly
___12. LUDICROUS   L. A first year player
___13. GROUSE   M. Shaky
___14. DANGLED   N. Twisting and bending out of shape
___15. RANDOM   O. Stopped
___16. MAMMOTH   P. Developing and hatching
___17. CHAOTIC   Q. Overjoyed
___18. SCANNED   R. Moving in a clumsy way
___19. COMMOTION   S. Complain; grumble
___20. PANDEMONIUM   T. Shabby and dirty
___21. SLEAZY   U. Ridiculous
___22. INCUBATING   V. Jeering
___23. SCOFFING   W. Uproar; confusion
___24. ROOKIE   X. Apparent; observable
___25. WRENCHED   Y. Looked over quickly

KEY: VOCABULARY WORKSHEET 2 - Mainac Magee

B - 1.	EXTORT	A. Disturbance
J - 2.	PERILOUS	B. To get by threats
R - 3.	BLUNDERING	C. Having no pattern or purpose
Q - 4.	ECSTATIC	D. Hung loosely
X - 5.	OBVIOUS	E. Gigantic; enormous
N - 6.	CONTORTIONS	F. To force open or up
G - 7.	ILLUSION	G. Fantasy; false belief
H - 8.	WRETCH	H. A miserable, unfortunate person
F - 9.	PRY	I. Twisted
M - 10.	RICKETY	J. Dangerous
O - 11.	HALTED	K. Disorderly
U - 12.	LUDICROUS	L. A first year player
S - 13.	GROUSE	M. Shaky
D - 14.	DANGLED	N. Twisting and bending out of shape
C - 15.	RANDOM	O. Stopped
E - 16.	MAMMOTH	P. Developing and hatching
K - 17.	CHAOTIC	Q. Overjoyed
Y - 18.	SCANNED	R. Moving in a clumsy way
A - 19.	COMMOTION	S. Complain; grumble
W 20.	PANDEMONIUM	T. Shabby and dirty
T - 21.	SLEAZY	U. Ridiculous
P - 22.	INCUBATING	V. Jeering
V - 23.	SCOFFING	W. Uproar; confusion
L - 24.	ROOKIE	X. Apparent; observable
I - 25.	WRENCHED	Y. Looked over quickly

JUGGLE LETTER REVIEW GAME CLUE SHEET 1 - Mainac Magee

1. YZLASE = 1. _____
   Shabby and dirty

2. ONERP = 2. _____
   Flat

3. LINIULSO = 3. _____
   Fantasy; false belief

4. TRTOINOSCNO = 4. _____
   Twisting and bending out of shape

5. DTEHLA = 5. _____
   Stopped

6. EVORGDNEC = 6. _____
   Came together

7. ETOSPRESPOUR = 7. _____
   Farfetched

8. ONGCSILW = 8. _____
   Wrinkling the forehead in anger

9. PESSALRRI = 9. _____
   Revenge

10. PTMRPO =10. _____
    Instant; immediate

11. MCERDAM =11. _____
    Crowded; packed

12. UVOIBSO =12. _____
    Apparent; observable

13. YPR =13. _____
    To force open or up

14. ALDGNED =14. _____
    Hung loosely

15. LCNOICOSSNU =15. _____
    End results

16. CMAANI = 16. _____
A person who has extra enthusiasm or desire

17. IDTGSI = 17. _____
Number symbols

18. NNPMAUEDMIO = 18. _____
Uproar; confusion

19. ARIGNNT = 19. _____
Speaking in a violent manner

20. UETLMNIY = 20. _____
Concerned with small details

21. OBDUDFDMUEN = 21. _____
Amazed; astonished

22. EATRGS = 22. _____
Parallel bars for blocking an opening

23. ITYERCK = 23. _____
Shaky

24. KYFNCII = 24. _____
Choosy; fussy

25. NWCEEDHR = 25. _____
Twisted

26. ENWOLIBLG = 26. _____
Yelling

27. ECDANNS = 27. _____
Looked over quickly

28. MMOHMTA = 28. _____
Gigantic; enomous

29. STCIECAT = 29. _____
Overjoyed

30. ISUOLDET = 30. _____
Aloneness

31. TSOREC = 31. _____
A guide or guard

32. NUETDNS =32. _____
Shocked

33. UXREBNACEE =33. _____
Enthusiasm

34. HIEXSUAOTN =34. _____
Complete weariness

35. VREELA =35. _____
Make known

36. RUETNDVE =36. _____
Went in spite of risk

37. UDOSCIURL =37. _____
Ridiculous

KEY: JUGGLE LETTER REVIEW GAME CLUE SHEET 1 - Mainac Magee

1. YZLASE = 1. SLEAZY
   Shabby and dirty

2. ONERP = 2. PRONE
   Flat

3. LINIULSO = 3. ILLUSION
   Fantasy; false belief

4. TRTOINOSCNO = 4. CONTORTIONS
   Twisting and bending out of shape

5. DTEHLA = 5. HALTED
   Stopped

6. EVORGDNEC = 6. CONVERGED
   Came together

7. ETOSPRESPOUR = 7. PREPOSTEROUS
   Farfetched

8. ONGCSILW = 8. SCOWLING
   Wrinkling the forehead in anger

9. PESSALRRI = 9. REPRISALS
   Revenge

10. PTMRPO = 10. PROMPT
    Instant; immediate

11. MCERDAM = 11. CRAMMED
    Crowded; packed

12. UVOIBSO = 12. OBVIOUS
    Apparent; observable

13. YPR = 13. PRY
    To force open or up

14. ALDGNED = 14. DANGLED
    Hung loosely

15. LCNOICOSSNU = 15. CONCLUSIONS
    End results

16. CMAANI =16. MANIAC
A person who has extra enthusiasm or desire

17. IDTGSI =17. DIGITS
Number symbols

18. NNPMAUEDMIO =18. PANDEMONIUM
Uproar; confusion

19. ARIGNNT =19. RANTING
Speaking in a violent manner

20. UETLMNIY =20. MINUTELY
Concerned with small details

21. OBDUDFDMUEN =21. DUMBFOUNDED
Amazed; astonished

22. EATRGS =22. GRATES
Parallel bars for blocking an opening

23. ITYERCK =23. RICKETY
Shaky

24. KYFNCII =24. FINICKY
Choosy; fussy

25. NWCEEDHR =25. WRENCHED
Twisted

26. ENWOLIBLG =26. BELLOWING
Yelling

27. ECDANNS =27. SCANNED
Looked over quickly

28. MMOHMTA =28. MAMMOTH
Gigantic; enomous

29. STCIECAT =29. ECSTATIC
Overjoyed

30. ISUOLDET =30. SOLITUDE
Aloneness

31. TSOREC =31. ESCORT
A guide or guard

32. NUETDNS =32. STUNNED
Shocked

33. UXREBNACEE =33. EXUBERANCE
Enthusiasm

34. HIEXSUAOTN =34. EXHAUSTION
Complete weariness

35. VREELA =35. REVEAL
Make known

36. RUETNDVE =36. VENTURED
Went in spite of risk

37. UDOSCIURL =37. LUDICROUS
Ridiculous

JUGGLE LETTER REVIEW GAME CLUE SHEET 2 - Mainac Magee

1. SOHDETI = 1. _____
   Lifted

2. EHGLUNSIDA = 2. _____
   Weakened; faded

3. UEGAV = 3. _____
   Unspecified; unclear

4. UGLINGN = 4. _____
   Moving forward suddenly

5. RUEVQI = 5. _____
   To shake with a slight movement

6. TINTSCISN = 6. _____
   Natural impulses or motivations

7. NETATUCLR = 7. _____
   Unwilling

8. HCGLIRUN = 8. _____
   Rolling or pitching suddenly

9. TIOCS = 9. _____
   Indifferent to pain or pleasure

10. EGDLZIRZ =10. _____
    Streaked with gray

11. TNPELAPARY =11. _____
    Easily understood

12. RATACUEC =12. _____
    Exactly correct

13. ERIPEXD =13. _____
    Ended

14. NGCATIINBU =14. _____
    Developing and hatching

15. DEURGS =15. _____
    Moved like waves

16. USEIPLOR =16. _____
Dangerous

17. MROAND =17. _____
Having no pattern or purpose

18. ENIFHLCD =18. _____
Shrank back in fear

19. NAVTAC =19. _____
Empty

20. NTOMCOOMI =20. _____
Disturbance

21. ERTHCW =21. _____
A miserable, unfortunate person

22. ITTSALYIB =22. _____
Dependability

23. SDAOOIENTL =23. _____
Gloom; bleakness

24. NGEIRBUNDL =24. _____
Moving in a clumsy way

25. OTIACHC =25. _____
Disorderly

26. UEERND =26. _____
To bear with tolerance

27. REPUSRUS =27. _____
Followers trying to overtake; chasers

28. EOFDNINC =28. _____
Limited

29. AFLTA =29. _____
Deadly

30. NGUAETTL =30. _____
An attack from all sides

31. UNOAMISF =31. _____
Having a very bad reputation

32. DCENELCH =32. _____
   Grasped tightly

33. TPNNOOEP =33. _____
   One against another

34. GCREIDN =34. _____
   Winced; recoiled

35. XOTETR =35. _____
   To get by threats

36. EINGHTSE =36. _____
   Violently excited

KEY: JUGGLE LETTER REVIEW GAME CLUE SHEET 2 - Mainac Magee

1. SOHDETI = 1. HOISTED
Lifted

2. EHGLUNSIDA = 2. LANGUISHED
Weakened; faded

3. UEGAV = 3. VAGUE
Unspecified; unclear

4. UGLINGN = 4. LUNGING
Moving forward suddenly

5. RUEVQI = 5. QUIVER
To shake with a slight movement

6. TINTSCISN = 6. INSTINCTS
Natural impulses or motivations

7. NETATUCLR = 7. RELUCTANT
Unwilling

8. HCGLIRUN = 8. LURCHING
Rolling or pitching suddenly

9. TIOCS = 9. STOIC
Indifferent to pain or pleasure

10. EGDLZIRZ =10. GRIZZLED
Streaked with gray

11. TNPELAPARY =11. APPARENTLY
Easily understood

12. RATACUEC =12. ACCURATE
Exactly correct

13. ERIPEXD =13. EXPIRED
Ended

14. NGCATIINBU =14. INCUBATING
Developing and hatching

15. DEURGS =15. SURGED
Moved like waves

16. USEIPLOR =16. PERILOUS
Dangerous

17. MROAND =17. RANDOM
Having no pattern or purpose

18. ENIFHLCD =18. FLINCHED
Shrank back in fear

19. NAVTAC =19. VACANT
Empty

20. NTOMCOOMI =20. COMMOTION
Disturbance

21. ERTHCW =21. WRETCH
A miserable, unfortunate person

22. ITTSALYIB =22. STABILITY
Dependability

23. SDAOOIENTL =23. DESOLATION
Gloom; bleakness

24. NGEIRBUNDL =24. BLUNDERING
Moving in a clumsy way

25. OTIACHC =25. CHAOTIC
Disorderly

26. UEERND =26. ENDURE
To bear with tolerance

27. REPUSURS =27. PURSUERS
Followers trying to overtake; chasers

28. EOFDNINC =28. CONFINED
Limited

29. AFLTA =29. FATAL
Deadly

30. NGUAETTL =30. GAUNTLET
An attack from all sides

31. UNOAMISF =31. INFAMOUS
Having a very bad reputation

32. DCENELCH =32. CLENCHED
Grasped tightly

33. TPNNOOEP =33. OPPONENT
One against another

34. GCREIDN =34. CRINGED
Winced; recoiled

35. XOTETR =35. EXTORT
To get by threats

36. EINGHTSE =36. SEETHING
Violently excited

www.ingramcontent.com/pod-product-compliance
Lightning Source LLC
Chambersburg PA
CBHW051405070526
44584CB00023B/3296